D1606307

Minister's Guidebook

Insights from a Fellow Minister

Dr. Glenn W. Mollette

Newburgh Press
Newburgh, Indiana
United States of America

For all the ministers, friends and a multitude of Christian people who helped and worked alongside me for many years. I would never have made it without your love, grace, perseverance and mercy. There are too many of you to name. Thank you so much for all you did to help me.

For all the dear family who have helped me along this journey. I love you and am more grateful for you than words can describe. Thank you so much for your love and support throughout the years.

Contents

Introduction

My hope in writing this book is to encourage and help you. Some or maybe a lot of this book may not even apply to you today, but some of it will. If all of this does not connect with you today, then save it for down the road because you might need this book later.

Throughout this book, I will come back and repeat a few scenarios that apply to different themes and situations. Old-time preachers have a habit of repeating illustrations, stories, and themes because we want to make sure you hear what we say.

This book contains about 50 years of pastoral, staff, and educational ministry service. I wrote this because I've been where you are or where you are going. You may be right there today. Hopefully, this book will give you some insights, affirmation, or a little light that will guide you, teach you, assure you, and encourage you.

Serving Jesus in ministry is the greatest work on the planet. In ministry, we are often trying to feel or think our way through different situations and scenarios. Maybe, these reflections and insights will shed some light on something that will help you today or later on in your ministry. If it doesn't help you some, then thank you anyway for taking the time to read this book. Consider passing this on to another minister.

You might consider having your church leadership read this book or teach it to some of your small groups. It might be eye-opening to them. God will have to lead you in this. In ministry, it is always important to be "wise as a serpent but harmless as a dove," Matthew 10:16.

For Jesus,

Glenn W. Mollette
July 18th, 2020
Very interesting - I was baptized on July 18th, 1970.
You never know what God can do over a period of 50 years.

Chapter 1

Your Ministry Age

"Now Jesus himself was about thirty years old when he began his ministry. He was the son, so it was thought, of Joseph," Luke 3:23

"Don't let anyone look down on you because you are young, but set an example for the believers in speech, in conduct, in love, in faith and in purity." 1 Timothy 4:12

"So, on that day Moses swore to me, 'The land on which your feet have walked will be your inheritance and that of your children forever, because you have followed the Lord my God wholeheartedly. Now then, just as the Lord promised, he has kept me alive for forty-five years since the time he said this to Moses, while Israel moved about in the wilderness. So here I am today, eighty-five years old! I am still as strong today as the day Moses sent me out; I'm just as vigorous to go out to battle now as I was then." Joshua 14: 9-11

"Count all the men from thirty to fifty years of age who come to serve in the work at the tent of meeting." Numbers 4:3

I was 15 years old when I prayed to receive Christ at a Vacation Bible School in Tomahawk, Kentucky. The Bible school was a mission Bible school sponsored by the First Baptist Church of Inez, Kentucky. They used an old Freewill Baptist Church building for the Bible school. At the time, they did not use the church building for anything. Since then, I understand it has been somewhat remodeled and is an active church.

A young teenage girl invited me to Bible school while I was playing baseball in her backyard with her brother and many other boys. Her dad had a large field behind his house. He graciously let his son and us have a baseball team that practiced many summer days in that field. My friend and his twin sister attended the Bible school along with several others and myself. Another high school friend, who was about 17 to 18 years old, and lived a couple of miles north of me on Milo Road, was the assigned teacher for a little group. My friend, his sister, and I sat in this class Monday through Friday. Several other teenagers and one other young adult who was a student at Georgetown College taught and led the Bible school. I rode my yellow Western Auto three-speed bicycle to Bible school for the five days.

When they invited me to the Bible school, they told me there would be snacks and games each day. That sounded okay, so I attended. It was interesting. Our teenage Bible teacher presented our group with a Bible lesson each day. On the last day, Friday, July 16th, she told the Bible story about the man who had lived a very successful life and built his barns and laid up his treasures for many years. He had reached a point where he essentially said, "I can take it easy now. I can eat, drink, and be merry." That day the man died. She told us that any of us could die suddenly. She also told the story about the rich man and Lazarus. Lazarus was a beggar who laid at the rich man's gate hungry and very sick. The rich man, who was not a man of faith in God, died and opened his eyes in hell. Lazarus died and was carried, by the angels, to heaven where he was comforted. The man who died without Christ spent an eternity suffering. Our teacher concluded that he is suffering there right now. She then explained how we could avoid an eternity in hell by accepting Christ as our Savior and putting our faith in him.

She asked the three of us if we would bow our heads. She explained if we would pray and invite Jesus into her our hearts that he would come into our hearts and lives to save us. She led us in prayer, and we had the option of praying silently. She then asked if any of us had prayed the prayer to raise our hands. We all three raised our hands. We had prayed to receive Christ.

I rode my bicycle home that July 16th day, about a three-mile ride, feeling pretty good. I certainly did not want to go to hell. I did love God and truly wanted to spend eternity in heaven. On Sunday morning, July 18th, I rode my bicycle to Inez. It was an extremely hot day. I put on the best clothes I owned, at that time, and rode the four-plus miles over two very big hills to get to town. I sat through the sermon and went forward, during the invitation, with several others who prayed to receive Christ in that mission Bible school. That evening, my mom and dad drove me to church and were with me as our group was baptized.

All the people who were involved in that mission Bible school were under 20 years old. The director was about 20. The teachers were all from 16 to 18. All of us who attended were 15 and under. I don't recall seeing anyone older than 20 the entire week. Most of the people who were in that Bible school became very productive citizens. They were active in their churches and two of us became ordained ministers.

What about age? Young people got the job done in that mission Bible school. They planned the Bible school. They conducted the Bible school. They invited people to the Bible school and effectively did the work of evangelism in that Bible school. The Bible school resulted in several baptisms and lifelong commitments of service to Christ from many of us.

I don't know when or if I would have become a Christian if I had not on that July day. My mother and father were Christians and were involved in church. At that point, I did not enjoy church at all. I thought church was extremely boring. I already had an innate respect for God and believed the Bible was a holy book. That had to come from living in a house where I heard a lot of Christian songs sung by mom and dad who were in a gospel quartet. My grandma and grandpa Hinkle were Godly people. My grandma had already prayed with me several times as a child. I feel like that, even as a young adult, I would have eventually responded to the gospel. However, I never, in my wildest dreams, ever imagined becoming a preacher of the gospel, pastoring churches, and spending my life in ministry. My interests were basketball and rock 'n' roll music. I still love sports today, and I love music, but Jesus is eternal. Everything is secondary and insignificant when it comes to Jesus and eternity.

After writing all the above, I now must share the following. Be careful about pushing it too quickly at a young age. I was ordained when I was 18 years old. I was pastoring two churches in my senior year of high school. I started preaching when I was 16. I pastored in high school, through college and seminary, and throughout most of my entire life. Altogether I have spent about 50 years in ministry and about 39 of them in pastoral ministry. I had a couple of brief stints in staff positions, but my ministry has mostly been pastoral. Looking back, I would wait a few years to serve as a pastor. If I could go back, I don't know if I would wait. Looking back, I can see if I had waited until I was about 27 or 28, I would have done a better job. The churches where I served did well. and we grew. They had money and good ministries. However, I know I could have done better if I had seasoned and matured a little before taking on such tremendous responsibilities.

Churches encourage youth to jump in and go. Youth should be encouraged. Youth inspire us when they want to be involved in the Lord's work. We should never discourage them from serving. If the old folks had poured cold water on my enthusiasm for the Lord, I might have walked away and given up. They encouraged me to preach and serve. That is the better choice. Most youth today are not being reached with the gospel message of Christ and are not connecting to the fellowship of the church. They desperately need to be connected.

Typically, once a person reaches adulthood without making a personal commitment to Christ, the chances become much slimmer for that person to ever commit to Christ and the church. If older children and teenagers hear the gospel and are given an opportunity, they are very likely to respond in faith. Most of the time, young believers in the gospel of Christ will hold this message of truth in their hearts throughout their lives. They may not always live the faith or may not act like persons of faith, but most of the time, they will hold the truth and the person of Christ in their hearts throughout their lives. Many adults, who embraced Jesus during childhood or their teenage years, will come back to the church, or at least recommit themselves to Jesus later in life.

Youth are enthusiastic. Youth inspire and attract others. Youth are beautiful. Yet, they will make mistakes. Youth are not emotionally prepared with life experiences or education. Youth want to take on adult responsibilities and learn along the way, but education is expensive. If the church people are not forgiving and helpful, then youth will burn out.

My high school chorus teacher got a little aggravated with me. She wanted me to do the narration for a Sunday afternoon performance. On Sunday afternoons, I was obligated to preach at the Liberty Baptist Church on the second and fourth Sundays of the month. She later had a little talk with me and told me that "I was taking on adult responsibility that I was not ready for and should not be doing." I was taken aback a bit by her candid comments, but I knew she was really perturbed that I bowed out of the school choral performance to go to a country church and preach.

A couple of weeks after that, she was preparing her awards for high school graduation and asked the high school chorus to vote on who should receive the male vocalist of the year award. The chorus members overwhelmingly voted for me. The teacher didn't like how the vote turned out. A week later, she asked everyone to vote again, and for the second time, the chorus elected me. She decided she was going to do what she wanted to do and gave two awards to two other guys in the class. Her actions toward me did not underscore any of her previously imparted wisdom. She simply made me feel that she was irritated with me. Not giving the award to me at graduation was her way of punishing me.

Looking back, I do not disagree with my chorus teacher's sentiments. I was too young to be doing all I was trying to do in ministry and pastoring churches. She was right. Her reasoning, her timing, and how she got back at me for not doing something she wanted me to do, did not speak well of her maturity. If I was wrong at the age of 18, her attitude, at the age of 40, was definitely wrong. We can be wrong at any age, and we can be right at any age.

Age is just a number. You serve when God calls you. God knows better than you. We've all read stories and heard of adults in their fifties and sixties who have made egregious mistakes. If you don't serve God as soon as he calls you to serve, you may not have the chance. I certainly had more preaching opportunities when I was younger than even now. Youth is always in demand. People are interested in what a young, dynamic, attractive person has to say. The doors open for youth. The problem with youth is not falling on your face or running out of steam. A 50 to 60-year-old minister has spent his or her life learning and understands that ministry and success require months and years. An older person understands the long haul of sermon preparation, dealing with personalities, and is not as likely to be in a hurry to push for ministry results.

In many ways, it would be ideal if all ministers could be mentored by someone up until they are 27 or 28. By the time they are 30 they have grown up some and are more ready to take hold of ministry maturely. A good pastor is wise to have many interns who he or she can disciple about the Lord's work and service. The interns are developing and growing. They are also building their resumes. They can point to their internship of one or two years, and they will have the senior pastor and fellow church members and fellow interns as references.

During these early years of young adulthood, at least a bachelor's degree could be completed and possibly a master's. I think we get in too big a hurry when it comes to the master's degree. There is nothing wrong with completing a master's degree in later years. I completed my Master of Divinity degree through Southern Baptist Theological Seminary, Louisville, Kentucky, when I was 25 years old. If I had not, I might not have ever finished the degree. So, the rule for education is to do the training when you can, and when it is available for you. Sooner is always better than later. Anything you put off may never happen.

However, education is now vastly different. Degree programs may be done at a different pace and are more about the student in some cases than the institution. I've seen thousands of ministers, between 40 and 90 years of age, completing first and second master's degrees, and even second doctoral degrees. Education and ministry should be an ongoing pursuit.

You may not live to old age. Serve Jesus while you can, even if you are 16. You may live to be 100. Wonderful! Think of all the time you will have to utilize all you have learned and know.

Chapter 2

Your Education

"Keep this Book of the Law always on your lips; meditate on it day and night, so that you may be careful to do everything written in it. Then you will be prosperous and successful." Joshua 1:8

"For Ezra had devoted himself to the study and observance of the Law of the Lord, and to teaching its decrees and laws in Israel." Ezra 7:10

"Hold on to instruction, do not let it go; guard it well, for it is your life." Proverbs 4:13

"Do your best to present yourself to God as one approved, a worker who does not need to be ashamed and who correctly handles the word of truth." 2 Timothy 2:15

"And the things you have heard me say in the presence of many witnesses entrust to reliable people who will also be qualified to teach others." 2 Timothy 2:2

"But in your hearts revere Christ as Lord. Always be prepared to give an answer to everyone who asks you to give the reason for the hope that you have. But do this with gentleness and respect," 1 Peter 3:15

"It is written: 'Man shall not live on bread alone, but on every word that comes from the mouth of God." Matthew 4:4

"The heart of the discerning acquires knowledge, for the ears of the wise seek it out." Proverbs 18:15

"The fear of the Lord is the beginning of knowledge, but fools despise wisdom and instruction," Proverbs 1:7

Do the best you can do. Obtain the best education you can obtain. Go to the school you can afford. Make the most of the school you attend. When it comes to education, you get out of it what you put into it.

Too many of us make education a dilemma. The truth is we don't need another dilemma. Education has become a financial albatross around the necks of too many people. Too many young adults are carrying school debt into their later years of life. There are cases where it is worth it to borrow tens or hundreds of thousands of dollars to go to school. If your education will enable you to earn enough money to live comfortably and pay back your school debt, then it makes sense. If your career produces only a modest income and it will require you to rake and scrap and forego meals because of school debt, then it does not make much sense.

People entering the medical field, whatever the specialty, are typically guaranteed opportunities to earn large enough salaries to pay back school debts. Even for these professions, it is not always easy. Many fields guarantee jobs for the person with a good education, work ethic, ability, and availability. Some of them pay more than others.

The person who aspires to be a public school teacher may not want to accumulate a mega debt. While teachers are paid better than ever and are deserving of all that they make, teaching is rarely a lucrative profession. It is a great profession, but school teachers seldom become rich. That means that you will need to carefully consider the school, the tuition rate, and how much you can afford for your education. You must also carefully consider how much money you can afford to borrow. Money borrowed is money that must be paid back. A large monthly payment, along with a car payment, rent payment, utility payments, telephone bills, and groceries, can be a strain on any budget. If that is what you want to do, and you feel it is necessary, then you can make it happen.

Ministerial education has become expensive right along with mainstream education. There was a time when the Southern Baptist Convention essentially trained all the ministers for free. When I attended Southern Baptist Theological Seminary in Louisville, Kentucky, from January 1, 1978, through May of 1980, there was no tuition but only some fees that they had started charging at that time. The fees were something like a couple of hundred dollars per semester. That was during the roaring era of the Southern Baptist convention right before the fracturing began to take place over the word "inerrancy." I was on campus for much of the denominational fiasco that was breaking out at that time. At that time, the convention was large and had lots of cash to support a large missionary force, six large campus seminaries, and many other entities. Financially underwriting the tuition of all the students attending all six Southern Baptist Theological Seminaries was truly an amazing accomplishment of the Southern Baptist Convention. I am truly grateful. All of us who benefitted from the generosity of God's people should ever be thankful.

That is one of the reasons that I have never turned my back on Southern Baptists. For many years, there has been a lot that I have not been thrilled about, but I still support several Southern Baptist Churches, and I am supportive of their Cooperative Program and mission efforts. I graduated from Seminary without any school debt. Southern Baptists made that possible, but I support ministries and churches who are not Southern Baptist as well. Although Newburgh Theological Seminary is interdenominational, I believe that it is important to remember those who helped us along in our journeys.

While attending First Baptist Church, Inez, Kentucky, I felt a call to ministry and, in particular, preaching ministry. By the time I was 16 years old, I had preached my first sermon at First Baptist, Inez. It was not long before I was preaching a lot for a 16-year-old. People love youth. Ministers, coaches, schools, communities, and almost all industries pump youth. If a young person has a talent or a drive to do something, they will be greatly encouraged in most cases. Most churches and pastors loved having a young preacher visit their pulpit. I was a high school student who had a lot to learn.

I started hearing a lot about Georgetown College, Georgetown, Kentucky. Georgetown is a four-year, liberal arts, traditional on-campus college. A student from First Baptist Inez attended Georgetown College, and his family was very high on the school. During high school, I made a couple of trips to the college campus. The school looked nice, and everyone was congenial. At this young age, I was visiting a college, trying to decide on something that would impact the rest of my life. The school offered a major in religion and communication, which I had an interest in pursuing.

The school was four years of class attendance. My junior year was spent at Wright State University outside of Dayton, Ohio. In the middle of attending Georgetown College, I went to Dayton, Ohio, to preach a revival one week in March in 1970. The pastor asked me to come and be his assistant for the summer, and I ended up staying in Dayton a couple of years where I married. During this time, I attended Wright State University and added classes to my Communications degree. In my senior year, I headed back to Georgetown College and commuted from Dayton, Ohio, to finish up the degree.

The rest of my traditional education continued at Southern Baptist Theological Seminary from January 1978 to May of 1980. My Master of Divinity program ended up being 84 hours of on-campus study. Overall, I loved Southern Seminary. The difference between Seminary and my liberal arts education at Georgetown was that I was finally studying what I wanted to study. In undergraduate, liberal arts colleges, so much time is spent on courses that often are not very interesting. Some of the classes you need and some of them, I am not so sure about. A school has an obligation to its accrediting group to offer what the accrediting group and administration of the school feel are necessary for a well-rounded and meaningful education. Certain classes are required for all majors regardless of whether they are English, religion, business, and so on. A lot of other classes that a student ends up taking require a lot of time and money. While these classes are necessary, typically, they have nothing to do with the student's pursued major.

I did my doctoral work at Lexington Theological Seminary, a Disciples of Christ seminary in Kentucky. Lexington was close to the church I was pastoring in Stamping Ground. They accepted me at the age of 26 to do the program. I completed the program at the age of 29 while pastoring First Baptist Church, Highland Heights, Kentucky. Up until I graduated from Lexington about all I had done my entire life was go to school and serve churches that were small enough or gracious enough to allow me to continue my education. That era was very different in comparison to what is now available through technology.

Would I do a three-year traditional seminary degree today? For the most part, it was enjoyable. After high school, I went through the rigors of an on-campus Bachelor's program, a Master's of Divinity Program, and a Doctoral program that took a big chunk out of my life. I started when I was 18 and finished when I was 29, with minimal breaks along the way. It was tough. I was married and had all of the financial pressures that go along with starting out as a young couple. I am sure I would still enjoy seminary classroom training and the fellowship of other students. Whether I would actually do it is another thing. The idea of commuting every day for 80 miles one way for classes and all the cost and inflexibility of an on-campus scenario probably would not work for me today. At the time, it was all that we had. We did what we had to do for training.

Today is different. The opportunities are greater than ever before. Technology, media, the Internet, email, and communications are all different and rapidly changing all the time. Classes can be done on your schedule and not on someone else's schedule. You can study when you have time or want to study. There are online classes that you can tune into at certain times, and there are still structured classroom settings that meet at certain times all over the planet. Online, self-paced studies require discipline and self-motivation.

Students should always do the best they can do when it comes to anything, particularly education. Up until about the age of 25 or 26, doing a traditional on-campus degree program is more realistically achievable. The older you become, life changes, and it gets much tougher. People marry, take on financial responsibilities, and generally begin being responsible for their housing and life's expenses. It becomes harder and harder as we age to sit in a classroom day after day. People do it through seminaries, medical schools, law schools, and many other graduate schools, often into their early thirties and beyond, but it is not easy. Typically, this is when students borrow thousands of dollars with perceived prospects of being able to pay back the loan. Education is never easy and is normally expensive.

Every person has to review his or her objectives very carefully. You have to balance out what you want and what it will take to accomplish what you want. If what you want requires three or four years of being on a campus and you can pull it off physically, financially, and emotionally, then, by all means, pursue your dream, accept the challenge and go forward. There are many cases where that is what you are required to do to have the profession you want and to achieve the salary level you desire.

When it comes to pastoring a church, you might spend three or four years at a traditional seminary, spend tens of thousands of dollars, and still never be hired or called to a church. Or, you may spend your life at small churches that may never enable you to have enough salary to pay back your loan. I am not saying this will happen to you, but it does happen.

Today, many churches are struggling. The possibility of graduating with a fulltime ministry waiting for you is not guaranteed. There are no guarantees. Many students want the assurance that if they earn a degree, from a certain school, they will be able to have the job they want. That will depend on the employer's job requirements. If you want a particular job, investigate what the employer expects. Then, consult with the employer and inquire as to whether you meet the requirements for the job you are seeking.

Lots of considerations go into job hiring, such as qualifications, work ethic, personality, aptitude for learning, working with others, and more. Do not ever think you can spend most of your life in a school, earn the graduate or doctoral degree of your dreams and then, simply have any job you want. You might. Your opportunities should be great, but you might not. One thing is certain, if you are trained, educated, prepared, and have a good academic background, it will not hurt you when you start sending out resumes. You will have a definite advantage.

Throughout my lifetime, I have known a lot of pastors who never finished college or maybe even only attended a semester of college or less. Most of the time, they were paranoid about their educational background and always made references in their sermons about, "When I was at college," or "I heard my professor say." More often than not, this was heard from preachers who attended very little college, than from preachers who spent years in seminary training. The ones who were actually trained, were not insecure and did not attempt to cover for their inadequacies.

Clergy are expected to have training. Congregations expect you have to have some academic/theological/ministerial training. However, if you are a people person with a hard work ethic and a willingness to study on your own, you can be successful, but you have to work harder.

A friend died a few years back, but I remember him as being one of the best at making it in ministry without any education.

He had one semester of college before he dropped out. He was a good communicator, and he learned early on that the preaching minister must spend a good part of his day in his study. He understood that good preaching required hours and hours of sermon preparation. He was always in a church that required three sermons a week on Sunday morning, Sunday night, and usually Wednesday evenings. He always gave the first four hours of his day to his reading and study time. He always did a good job when he preached. His pastorates were successful, and overall ministry went well throughout his entire life. His ministry was not the norm. A ministry like his happens, but I would never stake my career on it happening.

Anyone who wants a job should obtain the appropriate training credentials. Why should any church, nonprofit, or ministry organization hire you if you have not bothered to train for the job? When you present your resume, it should contain information that indicates that you have the training to do the job for which you are applying. Most churches or ministry groups will want someone with a minimum of a Bachelor's degree. A Master's degree is even better. Some entities will require someone who holds a degree from an institution within their denomination. A Methodist group may require someone from a Methodist seminary or a Baptist group may require someone from a Baptist seminary, and so on. I do not think this is the norm anymore. Churches are struggling so much today that they want someone who believes as they do and someone who can do the job. Someone who presents education credentials and demonstrates some previous success will have a chance of at least obtaining a second look and an interview. If you have nothing to put on your resume, then chances are nothing is going to happen for you.

The truth behind the ministry success of the man I mentioned earlier, applies to any preaching minister when it comes to daily schedules and study habits. When you graduate from school, your studying is not over but is just beginning a new era. If you are a preaching or a teaching minister at your church, you must spend hours undisturbed in your study. You cannot present good sermons or Bible studies if you try to study and prepare on the fly. Your study time has to be a top priority. If it isn't, when you go to the pulpit, you and the congregation will know you have not spent quality time preparing. The congregation may applaud you for all of your outreach, visiting, and running all over town shaking hands, but, your priority should be to present a good message on Sunday morning and whenever else the church meets. You cannot do it without quality, focused time, alone with God, in your study.

The minister's education is ever ongoing. You attend school to study, train, and prepare. After you graduate, you continue to study, train, and prepare, until your ministry is finished. It is a simple, yet a major part of your career. Study time must become a part of your daily routine. This has to be addressed upfront to the church and leaders so that everyone understands the importance of your regimented daily study time. They must understand it and respect your time, and the rewards should be mutual for you and the congregation.

Other ministry jobs will not require as many hours of focused study time for sermons and teaching. They do require planning and study. No ministry is exempt from spending time with God in prayer, reading the scriptures, planning, and organizing. Every ministry requires this if it is going to be successful.

Newburgh Theological Seminary and Newburgh College of the Bible began for people who could not attend a traditional four-year college or seminary. Our students are between 30 and 95 years old-this is no exaggeration. You would be surprised at the number of ministers in their eighties and nineties who are working on degrees. Some ministers live a long time and still want to do a disciplined study program and earn a degree for the time they have spent studying. Often, their rationale is that they study a lot anyway, so why not earn a degree for their time. That is a good rationale. We have had a lot of students from all 50 states and 40 countries who enroll in Newburgh to study and do further training from home.

A student enrolls in Newburgh or a school like Newburgh for numerous reasons. They do not have $80,000 or $150,000 or more to do an educational program. People in mid or late life need a program they can afford. Of course, who doesn't need a degree program they can afford? A $100,000 degree program is not an allurement to any age category. Most of our students already have a lot of life's responsibilities, families, careers, and need a program that works with their schedules.

Years ago, most colleges were committed to traditional, on-campus education. They debunked online and correspondence types of education as being inferior. Today, most of these institutions have changed their minds, have died, or are in the process of dying. The day of not being innovative when it comes to education has passed. There are fields of study where online/correspondence will not work. No one wants their surgeon to learn how to do surgery from a distance education school. He might complete some textbooks and papers online, but when it comes to learning and performing surgery, it must occur in an academic/medical setting. There are certainly other scenarios where the actual classroom setting is vital..

School is a lifelong process. You finish a degree, but then there is always more to learn if you are going to stay current. While you learn and retain a great deal from a degree program, you will need to refresh yourself in lifelong learning.

Wherever you go to school, and however you train, study to show yourself approved of God and rightly divide the word of truth.

Chapter 3

Your Study Time

Every minister needs daily time for Bible reading, prayer, study, and time to think about what he or she is reading.

Life is busy. It is easy to occupy your mind with busy thoughts. Often, our minds are occupied, with many thoughts that pull us in different directions. Cares, family, health, finances, life's needs, and goals can be exhausting. The minister who goes to the pulpit every week to deliver a sermon must have time every day to prepare for the occasion. Anyone who waits until Saturday night to throw together a quick outline is going to come up short when it is time to stand up and deliver.

Whether you are a senior preaching pastor or a staff minister who teaches the youth, senior adults, or children, study time applies to all teachers of the gospel. All age groups are important, and everyone needs time to read and organize their thoughts. However, if your job is mostly to preach the gospel on Sunday morning and for other services, then your priority has to be your study.

Today, it is easier than ever to come up with good sermon material from the Internet. Many famous and great preachers have their sermons online. They are easy to print out or even copy their notes and paste to read right off a manuscript. I am not advocating plagiarism. However, to some extent and on some level, we have all been there. We have used illustrations and outlines that we have heard or read from others. We have used material from others and forgotten to acknowledge that the material we were presenting was not necessarily original. The fact is there is very little, if anything, that is entirely original.

The news stories of the day are new and original as we use them to intertwine into our sermons. However, we do not create news stories. We pluck them off the latest news feed or television headline. While we are using the news headline, thousands of other preachers are probably doing the same thing. So, the story is not something original we claim, but we utilize the story to proclaim the word of the Lord. The words of Jesus are his words. They don't belong to us. However, Jesus told us to go out into the world and tell the good news. His good news. Jesus wants us to talk about him. His stories. His life. His Parables. His miracles. His death, burial, and resurrection from the grave. The stories of the Bible are old stories. They have all been told millions and millions of times. We hope they are told millions more times. Our job is to read the Bible, study books, and reference material that give us insights into the Bible, and then tell the story of the Bible.

The only way we can do a good job of teaching or telling the stories of the Bible is to read the Bible. Memorize the Bible. Apply the Bible to our lives and the current times of our world. Then, put together a message that is 20 to 30 minutes in length that succinctly delivers all that you have read and thought about. It is more difficult to deliver a good 20 to 30-minute sermon than to chase rabbits for an hour. Some preachers get up and go on and on about one thing and then another, twisting here and there, and wear us out. It is easy to get up and kill time talking about whatever comes into your mind. The proof of a studied, prepared preacher is a sermon that has a message. A good message is hammered and chiseled out in the early morning hours in the quiet sphere of wherever the minister meets with God and his holy word.

You may not have an elaborate study. Any place will do. Convenience and what is practical are always best. Many ministers set up studies in their homes. Some wait until they arrive at their office. I have done both. If you can go right from your bed with your coffee or breakfast drink to your study, you will accomplish more. That makes God and studies first. Normally, when you first get out of bed, you are fresher. Try to get up one to two hours before everyone else. If you have small children, they are sleeping. Your spouse is still resting. The television and other sounds are quiet. Use this hour or two to read without rushing.

Meet God when there is no one else to distract from what he is saying to you. Use this time to memorize the Bible, reflect, digest the scripture, and then read some of the headlines for the day. Prayerfully consider how these headlines and God's word mesh and what God is saying to you about today. Often, in these quiet moments, you will be startled by some of the amazing insights you will have. You will be surprised by the themes, ideas, and scriptural enlightenment of God's word that you will have.

If you are exhausted, you don't think well. You don't read well. You don't retain well, and your ideas are sparse. That is why late-night study and sermon building is often very difficult. You have waited until the very last minute of the day to meet with God, and you are too tired for God. You are too tired for anything.

We've all been there. I've crammed for sermons too many times to remember. I remember there wasn't anything fun or fulfilling about putting off my sermon preparation until the last minute, and then throwing it together. I started preaching when I was 16. I knew nothing about preaching or ministry. Most of what I have learned, I have learned the hard way. Education is always expensive. Finally, I learned that sermon building starts early. Build your theme for several weeks in advance. Themes change and develop as events and the news change, but you have direction as to where you are going. That is why many ministers preach through books of the Bible or develop different series that follow the calendar as they plan sermons to coincide with seasons and dates.

Many ministers follow the newspaper headlines, and study in accordance with what is going on during the day. There is always breaking news. There is always a new headline. Many ministers tie the headlines of the day into their latest sermon. That is not a bad way to preach because people are already tuned into the theme of the day. When you start talking, they immediately know what you are talking about. You immediately have their interest because it's a news story. As you launch into the story and incorporate scripture, you are helping your congregation to see how the Bible and Jesus are relevant to their lives.

However you preach, whatever you preach, however long you preach, however many times a week you preach, and especially how well you preach will depend on one thing. That one thing is how much of your life you have given to your message. Every sermon requires a piece of your heart. There is no sermon worth preaching that did not take some of your heart out and put it on the altar for God. In Luke 8:46 we read, "But Jesus said, 'Someone touched me; I know that power has gone out from me." Jesus felt something go out of him as a woman in need of healing touched him. She reached out to Jesus believing that Jesus could help.

Every Sunday and throughout the week, you have people reaching out to you as a minister. You will see it in their faces. You will hear it in their questions. You will experience it in their cries for help. "Pastor, please come to the hospital. Please come to the funeral home. Please talk with me, my marriage is dying. Please help me with my drug addiction," and so much more. The minister pours himself into other people and situations. God's strength cannot be poured out if you have not stored up that strength by spending enough time with God. If you aren't careful, your spiritual tank will run dry as you spend your time doing everything other than fueling your soul. If you are on empty when people touch you, call on you, jostle you, aggravate you, trouble you, question you, malign you, throw rocks at you, what will you have to give to them? Too often, we are running on fumes, or we are empty with little or nothing left to give.

Jesus spent a lot of time with the Father. We read in Mark chapter 1: 35-37 "It was very early in the morning and still dark, Jesus got up and left the house. He went to a place where he could be alone. There he prayed. Simon and his friends went to look for Jesus. When they found him, they called out, "Everyone is looking for you!" From here, Jesus went out to preach and do the work the Father had sent him to do. In the next verses, we see him traveling all around Galilee and preaching in the synagogues. Jesus spent time alone so that he might prepare himself to preach to others and do the ministry he came to do. Again, in Luke 6: 12-13, we read, "One of those days Jesus went out to a mountainside to pray, and spent the night praying to God. When morning came, he called his disciples to him and chose 12 of them, whom he also designated apostles." Before Jesus chose his 12 disciples, he spent the night in a quiet place. The people he surrounded himself with, in his ministry, were very important. Jesus wanted to have time alone praying to God throughout the night before he made such a selection.

There are other occasions where Jesus sought a quiet place to pray, be alone with God, and to prepare himself. Another occasion is found in Luke 22: verses 39-44, "Jesus went out as usual to the Mount of Olives, and his disciples followed him. On reaching the place, he said to them, 'Pray that you will not fall into temptation.' He withdrew about a stone's throw beyond them, knelt down, and prayed, "Father, if you are willing, take this cup from me; yet not my will but yours be done. An angel from heaven appeared to him and strengthened him. And being in anguish he prayed more earnestly, and sweat was like drops of blood falling to the ground."

The most agonizing time in Jesus' life was coming. His arrest, trial, and crucifixion. No human would ever face what Jesus faced. In ministry, we go through a lot. We will all face trials, and even agonizing moments in life. Life is filled with pain and sorrow. If you live long enough, you will face trials. Jesus did all he knew to do to prepare for what he would face. That was spending time alone with the Father in fervent prayer. If Jesus needed time alone with the Father, surely, so do we.

You will accomplish more, write better sermons, feel better, know more, and feel as if you know God a little better if you meet him early, in a quiet place. Whenever and wherever you have your study and quiet time, the main thing is to do it often. If you do it at home and early in the morning, you can do it every day. Having to get in your car and drive to the church or another location only kills time that you could be using to read, pray, or accomplish something. However, every situation is a bit different. Do what works best for you and God. Schedules, living arrangements, energy levels are different for all of us. The main thing is to meet God routinely, have time alone with him. Be able to focus, be quiet, study, pray, and reflect during the time that you set aside. You will be stronger, better equipped to preach, teach, and serve. Your ministry will be a much more enjoyable ministry.

Chapter 4

Your Marriage

"And over all these virtues put on love, which binds them all together in perfect unity," Colossians 3:14

"For husbands, this means love your wives, just as Christ loved the church. He gave up his life for her," Ephesians 5:25

"Therefore, a man shall leave his father and his mother and hold fast to his wife, and they shall become one flesh," Genesis 2:24

"Though one may be overpowered, two can defend themselves. A cord of three strands is not quickly broken," Ecclesiastes 4:12

"Two are better than one, because they have a good return for their labor: If either of them falls down, one can help the other up. But pity anyone who falls and has no one to help them up. Also, if two lie down together, they will keep warm. But how can one keep warm alone?" Ecclesiastes 4:9

"With all humility and gentleness, with patience, bearing with one another in love, eager to maintain the unity of the Spirit in the bond of peace." Ephesians 4:2-3

Mark 10:9: "Therefore what God has joined together, let no one separate."

Ephesians 5:25-33: "Husbands, love your wives, as Christ loved the church and gave himself up for her, that he might sanctify her, having cleansed her by the washing of water with the word, so that he might present the church to himself in splendor, without spot or wrinkle or any such thing, that she might be holy and without blemish. In the same way husbands should love their wives as their own bodies. He who loves his wife loves himself. For no one ever hated his own flesh, but nourishes and cherishes it, just as Christ does the church, ..." Ephesians 5: 25-33

"Owe no one anything, except to love each other, for the one who loves another has fulfilled the law," Romans 13:8

"Love is patient, love is kind. It does not envy, it does not boast, it is not proud. It does not dishonor others, it is not self-seeking, it is not easily angered, it keeps no record of wrongs," 1 Corinthians 13:4-5

"If I have the gift of prophecy and can fathom all mysteries and all knowledge, and if I have a faith that can move mountains, but do not have love, I am nothing."

"Do everything in love," 1 Corinthians 16:14

"Many waters cannot quench love; rivers cannot wash it away. If one were to give all the wealth of his house for love, it would be utterly scorned," Song of Solomon 8:7

"Let the morning bring me word of your unfailing love, for I have put my trust in you. Show me the way I should go, for to you I entrust my life," Psalm 143:8

"Let love and faithfulness never leave you; bind them around your neck, write them on the tablet of your heart. Then you will win favor and a good name in the sight of God and man," Proverbs 3: 3-4

You may be married or have plans to marry. Maybe you are not married and do not plan to marry. You may be recently widowed or even divorced.

A good marriage will be a blessing. A bad one is like having an albatross around your neck and being thrown into a lake. There is nothing greater or better than a life marriage partner. On the other hand, it would not be good to live in a relationship where the marriage is bad.

Expectations, whether reasonable or unreasonable, moods, health issues, external pressures, finances, parents, children, your jobs, and so on, go into the mix of determining how your marriage is going. Job pressures, financial problems, intrusive parents, care of parents, sickness, a troubled child, and many more can twist and turn the very best of God's good people.

When you marry someone, you enter the relationship with all the hopes, dreams, possibilities, and a vision for a better life and a better future. No one enters a marriage hoping that the relationship has a bad or negative future. You are looking toward the future with new hope and dreams. If anyone ever marries thinking in the beginning that this might be a bad idea, then getting married is a bad idea. Often people marry thinking they can change a person or cure a person or straighten a person out. People are not changed by signing a marriage license. However, people do change after marriage.

Marriage should be about two people, in love, committing themselves to each other in hopes of a better life, not one that is worse.

All of the above holds true for the minister. No spouse enters into a marriage for his or her life to become hell on earth. Marriage is about love, flowers, candy on Valentine's day, holding hands, sexual intimacy, cleaning up the kitchen, vacuuming the carpet, dusting the furniture, shaking the rugs, and sharing peacefully about 1000 meals or snacks together throughout the year. The number of shared meals drops way down in many cases when both marriage partners have careers outside the home. They may be fortunate if they are eating one meal together a day. If you are not careful, mealtime spent together can drop way down,

When you marry someone, it is not for the career that he or she holds. Sometimes, people do that, but it is a bad idea because jobs change. People change jobs, lose jobs, or sometimes develop other interests and change careers. It is the same way in ministry. Some ministers may stay with a church for 30 years but may change churches every two or three years. Moving from town to town and from parsonage to parsonage is tough. You may have a really good ministry, or you may have some ups and downs in your ministry. Most likely, you will experience a combination of both.

Every problem that the minister and the church face usually ends up in the minister's home. Often, the stress of whatever is happening at church is felt by the pastor or ministry staff person. Married people are going to talk about problems. That often causes stress, concern, or outright worry as to how the issue at church is going to work out. When you are a minister, the church is your life and ends up being the life of your spouse and kids. You are not just there eight hours a day and then done. Typically, your spouse is there with you on Sundays and often has roles in the church as well. The kids are also involved. The entire family is caught up in the life of the church. Often this can be a great thing. The kids are involved in children's activities or youth activities. There are women's events going on almost all the time as well as functions for the men. Most of the time, this provides a wonderful opportunity, for the family to be together, grow together, and do something together. The family that prays together, goes places together and does things together typically stays together.

When you marry, you do not marry the church. Many ministers miss this one. Catholics look at this differently because priests are essentially married to the church. They do not marry wives. They marry the church. Sometimes, protestant churches get this wrong. In theory, you are married to a person. Too often, people in your congregation expect the church to come first. Too many ministers are married to the church, and they live with a spouse who they only see occasionally. They have a legal document that says they are married to a woman or a man with whom they live. However, most of their lives are spent at the church, studying, going to meetings, attending funerals and weddings, visiting hospitals and nursing homes, and trying to grow the church or keep it going. Ministers must get this right early on. God is first, your spouse and family are second and your church or job is third. You serve God, and you are serving the congregation, but you have a wife or husband. Your family is your first priority. That does not mean that you skip preaching on Sunday to attend your son's softball game. You do have a job you are being paid to do.

Ministry leaders and churches mess up when they do not designate a day, during the week, as the minister's day off. Many try to make Saturday a day off, and that day should be free, especially if you have children and events to attend with your children. However, if you are a teaching or preaching minister you never really have a Saturday off because you are always thinking about the sermon or the lesson to be taught on Sunday. If you can have your scripture and message or lesson internalized and ready to speak for Sunday by Friday, then you will feel freer on Saturday to do things with your family. However, by early Saturday evening, you have to turn off the television and media devices and refocus on what you had finished preparing on Friday. There is nothing worse than a minister cramming and scurrying on Saturday night for a message to present for

Sunday morning. Plan your sermons out weeks in advance. On Monday, begin building the message for Sunday. Take Tuesday or Thursday for just you and your spouse if possible, and keep your evenings as free as possible for your children. The church should schedule their meetings for Sunday afternoons or early evening or on Wednesdays and not tie up every day of the week. When meetings are scheduled for three or four nights a week for the minister to attend, it is a strain on family life for everyone.

I have been in churches that had so many meetings it became obvious that some of the people in the meetings simply didn't want to be at home. That is not healthy for the minister or the families of the people involved in the meetings.

When I married, I had been in ministry for over four years. Pastoral ministry and preaching had already been a consuming passion. I practically gave up high school basketball, playing in a rock 'n' roll band, and most everything else to fulfill what was a compelling internal call from God to preach and do the work of a minister. I have done it in some capacity for 50 years. Along the way, I had brief stints in church staff roles. For the most part, I have been the pastor of a church for about 40 of these 50 years. Serving in different capacities of Christian education for the last 20 years, plus pastoring a church for several of those years, has been a different form of service and internal calling. It has been very gratifying as well to work with so many of God's wonderful called servants.

The point is, when we married, my wife was marrying someone called and committed to ministry. I loved preaching and would rather have preached than anything else. I laid everything down to preach the gospel, including my basketball and guitar, which I loved and still enjoy today. However, I would have enjoyed a career in sports or music, and probably would have done okay in some aspect of either, but my passion was preaching. Today, nothing is different, I still hear the trumpets as I have the opportunity to be a guest speaker, preach for one of our students, or share the gospel of Christ in any setting. When my first wife and I married she knew she was marrying a Baptist preacher. She loved the church. She had a major in music and had trained her entire life to play the piano. She was the best I have ever heard.

If you are married and make a decision to enter the ministry, you and your spouse need to sit down and talk long and hard about what it involves. That can be a great new adventure and very rewarding for both of you. Doing God's work, winning people to Christ is the greatest work in the world. Some of the happiest people I know on the planet are couples sharing and doing God's work together. However, if you both are not on board, you will have problems. You will struggle if you are at church most of the time, and your spouse is left to do something else most of the time. Some marriages make it work. I know of one couple who are both pastors. The man has a congregation, and his wife has a congregation on the other side of town. They are in opposite directions on Sundays and other days but come home to each other. He has his job. She has her job. That is a scenario that can work, but like any situation, you have to know what is going on. His church understands. Her church understands. They both understand, and, therefore, it works.

As people and churches clarify expectations, goals, and parameters, then there is a better chance for success. A sure failure for any pastor/church relationship is when the expectations are unclear, and more and more is expected all the time. Normally, ministers can deal with what they know is expected of them. However, it is much more difficult to handle the curves that are thrown. Yet, life is filled with curves and surprises that must be handled with wisdom and caution.

Many marriages do great in ministry. Husbands and wives enjoy the work of the Lord together. Vocationally, spiritually and even, recreationally the church becomes your life. You will need to find days to get out of town, go to the lake, and participate in activities that aren't solely church-related. However, the minister's family will spend most of their lives in the activities of the church. Overall this will be rewarding as you will always have something to do. You will never have a week wondering what you are going to do with your time. Your week of church-related functions will mostly be planned for you. Of course, this will not include the surprise funerals and crises that come about in your community that will require your attention. Community happenings will be ongoing all the time. One year I led the opening invocation for almost every college basketball game in our town. That was not a major event, but it was someplace to go, something to do, and a place to be seen as the local pastor of the church. Often you will be called upon to fill up your schedule with activities that are okay to do. Throughout your ministry, you will make a lot of choices between what is good and what is best. There will be a lot of good services and ministry you can render, but often you will have to determine if it is the best use of your time in your ministry. Only God, you, and your spouse can determine this.

You do not have to be married to be a minister. Jesus was not married. If you are not married, you can make it work to your advantage because you can almost be married to the church. A lot of churches or ministries may not even consider hiring an unmarried person, but the person without a family has a lot more time to devote to sermon preparation, hospital visits, pastoral care, listening to others, prayer, outreach, and much more. You may not have a spouse to share the joy with, but you do not have someone who may be crying about how much you are away from the house, or how much pressure they feel from church members, or about how little money there is to live on. Let's pause here and stress that just because you are single does not mean that you are to be married to the church. You must have a day off and time to yourself the same as a married minister. There have to be limitations on text messaging, responding to the telephone, and being on call all the time. Everyone must have time when they are not on the clock and expected to be working. No one can work 24/7. There must be times when you can turn the cell phone off and be off duty. That applies to all areas of ministry regardless of marital status.

A minister's home can be a joyful place, but it can be a stressful place if the ministry has overbearing expectations and meager pay to compensate for all the expectations.

Some congregations expect their ministers to be humble and poor. "God you make our minister humble, and we will make him poor," is sometimes the sentiment. That puts a huge amount of stress on any family if this is the sentiment of the church leadership.

The minister and spouse determine the marriage. Marriage is between two people. You cannot and should never marry for any other reason except for your desire to be with your mate. You cannot and never should marry because it would be good or better for your ministry. If you marry for that reason, then it will end up not being good for your life. It is your life that produces your ministry. Your ministry is an overflow of your life. If your life is not joyful and solid, then your ministry is not going to be joyful. You cannot help your church to be joyful if you are miserable. Some ministers do a good job of it for a while. They keep going. They keep a good face and say and do the right things. After a while, whatever is internal will become external. Marry for love and make the marriage about you and your spouse and not about anybody else. Your ministry and everyone touched by your ministry will be blessed by you and your marriage.

Keep your congregation out of your marriage. That is easier said than done. You and your spouse will make friends with people in your church. The longer you are in one church, the more people you will know. Do not confide any marital problems or stresses to people in your congregation. Whatever you tell will be retold and retold and retold. You do not need to live out your marital disagreements, problems, or tensions with your congregation. That will only make the issue seem larger than it is. Soon you will have people in your church who will be calling or coming around interested in talking to you, pretending to be your friend so they can hear more about your problem.

Keep your marriage between you and your spouse. That doesn't mean that you can't talk to anybody else about your marriage partner or your marriage. Keep in mind that in most cases, when you talk about your wife or husband to anyone else, you are probably talking to a larger audience. People repeat what the pastor says or what the spouse of the pastor says. They especially repeat it if it is negative. Keep your dirt swept up and put away. No one needs to see your dirty laundry. That does not mean you and your spouse shouldn't take care of your problems. You should work it out between the two of you, without involving the rest of the community.

Beware of extended gossip sessions that are disguised as "prayer" sessions. It is great to gather for prayer. When the prayer meeting turns into a long, extended talk, everyone is "sharing", tears are falling, and people are hugging each other, that is when people start loosening up and feeling like they can talk about anything and everything. You and your spouse may think, "these people are my friends" and "these people love me."

So, you start talking too much and sharing too much personal information. Keep in mind that you have told the world, and there isn't anything those people can do except divide and destroy your marriage. It will not take long for someone or several in that group to attach themselves to you because they have similar issues. Before you know it, you are talking more to them than you are your husband or your wife. What happens is that you start believing they "care" more or "understand" more than your marriage partner. You develop a connection, and the phone calls and messages flow every day. That will steal time away from you and the time you need to be with your spouse. If you do have a problem in your home, you cannot go outside your home to fix the problem. The problem is an inside job that only you and your spouse can fix together with God's help.

At one time or another, everyone may need someone to talk with, but often, it is difficult. If you and your spouse need counseling, you should drive two or three hours away and talk to a real counselor who is not part of your community.

Pastors have lunch meetings or coffee gatherings with other ministers. That is not the place to talk about marital issues you have. Some ministers do gossip and have a network of other ministers to whom they tell everything.

A friend of mine said, "When you tell something bad it will be repeated and not for your good but for your bad."

Normally, two people can work out almost anything. If it is something you cannot work out, in the quiet confines of your own home, between the two of you and the guiding hand of God, then you may need a professional. Professional counseling may help to resolve the problem, but it may not. Sometimes when it gets to that point, all the professional does is further encourage more talk about the problems without directing you to peace, reconciliation, and a happy marriage. If there is an issue and you have talked openly to each other, prayed, worked together, sought God's wisdom, and even sought professional help, then there comes a time when you have to move on. You move forward and beyond and decide between each other, and with God's help, you are going to go forward. If you are unable to do that, then you are in trouble.

The single minister should never feel pressured to marry to get or keep a ministry. Your life is bigger than any job, church, or ministry. A single pastor told me about being engaged and deciding he could not go through with the marriage, and he broke it off. The girl he was engaged to, was a member of his church. Her family and friends were members of his church. Several months after he broke off the engagement, he resigned from his church under pressure and had to look for another ministry. Thus, if you are a single minister, be wary of dating anyone in your church. Sometimes it works out. Another pastor I know dated and then married a lady in his church, and it worked out beautifully. Sometimes it does, and sometimes it does not. If it works out, it's beautiful. If it ends sourly, then other people in the church get caught up in the breakup, and there will be discord that the minister and the church do not need. Prayerfully consider whether it is worth the risk before you date someone in your congregation. If it is, then go for it but make sure you fully understand the potential ramifications.

We all know of ministers' marriages that have failed. We know of big-name preachers who have gone through a divorce and pastors of smaller churches who have divorced. No home is immune. No minister and spouse begin a marriage with the intention of divorcing. I have never met anyone who stood at the altar and said their wedding vows with a plan in mind to divorce whoever they were marrying. Maybe it happens, but that is not common. Marriage is something that two people generally want and mutually agree on. However, as we know, sometimes people marry because they feel like they have to. Women have gotten pregnant and have felt pressured to marry. That does not happen like it used to. Once upon a time, if a single girl became pregnant, she, her family, and everyone felt like she had to marry as soon as possible. That does not happen as much anymore. Two wrongs do not make a right. You should never marry a person out of coercion or a feeling of obligation. Being a single parent is tough and has lots of hardships. It is still better than marrying the wrong person and trying to raise a child with the wrong person. Enter marriage with love and hope for a better life and a better future.

No one in his or her right mind should marry a person anticipating that life is going to be worse or terrible. You marry believing the two of you can live under the same roof in harmony.

You marry believing the two of you can have a life that is better together than apart. The person you are marrying is who you will share your bed, your table, your sofa, your kitchen, your car, and your bathroom with for the rest of your life. You will be together in sickness and health, poverty and wealth, good times and bad, and much more. It is a vitally important decision made between two people who join together and then spend the rest of their lives together for better or worse.

The minister and spouse who divorce go through trauma as all do who divorce. I do not think I have ever heard of an easy, painless divorce. Most are tough to some extent. When children are involved and devastated by a divorce, it is especially traumatic. When the minister divorces, the entire congregation and community are caught up in the dissolution. If you are living in a church-owned home, then everybody will be moving out very soon. If you own your own home, then eventually someone will be moving out. If you have children, it won't be your children. Spiritually, emotionally and even physically, everyone is devastated by the separation. Divorce does not create an overnight scenario for better health. However, if you are living in an abusive, bad marriage, your health is bound to improve.

As a minister, no one will want to hire you in a ministry position for a while. Some congregations will never employ a divorced minister. Today, more churches will hire you than ever before, but they probably will want to hear the story of why, in your opinion, the divorce occurred. There are always two sides to any divorce, and usually, everyone plays a role when a marriage fails. A good marriage takes two people. Generally, both people contribute, in some way, to the demise of a marriage.

Some ministers change denominations after a divorce. Some connect to interdenominational or non-denominational churches. Some start their own church knowing that is the only way that they will ever have a ministry again. Some are smart to work secular jobs for a while and let the emotions and pain of the divorce level out. It is difficult to minister to anyone if you are in personal pain. There are typically always sales jobs in larger towns and communities. You have to do something and whatever it takes to pay your apartment rent or housing costs. If you are able, you might consider trying to find a job that requires physical work like a factory or something in retail that keeps you moving. Mentally, you will feel better if you can do something that requires some physical exertion during the day. In time, God will work it out for you to have another ministry position, if you want one, and you are spiritually and emotionally healed, and things are resolved in your heart and life to do God's work. That is a painful process. You will find out who your real friends are and who they are not. You and your friends will always be a little surprised by both. The real friends who appear will be the ones who will throw you a lifeline and prevent you from drowning. The ones who you thought were your friends will be hard to find. Sometimes even the people who you thought were your very best friends will say and do things to hurt you.

Everyone suffers when a minister divorces. The spouse has to find housing or resolve housing issues. There is nothing but a valley of stress, pain, tears, loneliness, and fear down the path of divorce. The road to eventual peace and feelings of wholeness again will be a journey of prayer, discovery, and rebuilding your life all over again.

My first wife Karen passed away after a traumatic 12-year struggle with multiple sclerosis. I have written a lot about her illness and our struggles with the long process of that disease in my books Silent Struggler and Nursing Home Nightmares. I have also mentioned her in different ways in my Spiritual Chocolate series of books. Death and divorce are similar and then, of course, far different. They both are the end of a marriage. I have heard people say they thought it would have been much easier if their husband or wife had died instead of them having to go through a divorce. Divorce is bad, financially tough, and socially devastating, but there is life after divorce. Keep in mind that divorce is better than murder. Ruth Graham, the wife of Billy Graham, once was asked if she had ever thought about divorce. She replied, "Divorce no. Murder yes!" Of course, she said that as a joke, and it is always repeated as a joke.

When Karen passed away, I was at an emotional 12-year low. I was depleted. My sons Jared and Zachary were 20 and 17. For 12 cruel years, they watched their mother's health fail. They loved their mother. They suffered as boys, teenagers, and young adults. They saw their mother suffer and felt the heaviness of an insidious disease that would not stop or slow down until it sucked the very life out of her. They watched me suffer, juggle to keep our family together, pray, cry, and do everything I could do to try to save Karen, help her, and make her life better. With a progressive disease like MS, it is a daily battle. The person who suffered the most was Karen. Multiple sclerosis is cruel and unrelenting.

Amazingly, our church flourished during the ten years that I was their pastor. We grew by adding people to the church almost every Sunday. Financially, our giving was fantastic. We gave more to missions than the church had ever given. We built an incredible new facility. We expanded the staff. It was a great ministry.

Karen passed away on November 18, 2002. We talked and cried about everything. She told me more than once that I had to go on and live my life. That is never an easy thing to do. During our conversations, I told Karen that I would have to resign from Gateway Baptist Church if she died. I knew the church would never let me stay as a single minister nor would they like it if I dated and remarried. I knew that when she died, my ministry would be over at Gateway. I was right.

A little over two years later, I married Carole Bartley on January 8th, 2005. Karen and I had known Carole since our days at Stamping Ground Baptist Church in Scott County, Kentucky. We met Carole when I was 24 years old. When Carole and I married, I was two days shy of being 50 years old. Carole's first marriage had failed, and she went through a divorce. She had three daughters from her first marriage. Carole had been a friend to Karen for many years, but we had not seen her or her family for about nine years.

When Carole started occasionally attending Gateway Baptist Church, it raised some eyebrows. When she sat with me at a church dinner, there were more eyebrows raised. When we started dating, a small faction of the church leadership utilized our dating as an excuse to criticize everything about me. It is amazing how people change. One minute they are crying with you and praying with you, and the next minute they want you out of their sight.

As predicted, I knew that after Karen's death my departure from the church would come, but the reality of living through it was tougher than I had expected. Leaving all I had known for ten years added a further emotional setback for me and also my sons after burying my wife and their mother.

For the ten years that Karen was sick, we wept and struggled, the church wept and prayed, and we grew. When I decided I would try to stop crying, move forward and be happy, the congregation did not like that person near as much as the person who was desperate before God every week hoping and praying for a miracle. It is interesting what motivates people and what causes people to support you. Overall, people reach out to us and try to support us when we are hurting and desperate. If we are happy and doing well people are not as apt to rally around us.

Karen was a beautiful lady, but disease, like multiple sclerosis, takes its toll on our bodies. The physical body diminishes and wastes away to the disease and treatments of the disease.

Carole is a beautiful lady. If I had started dating and married one of the church member's daughters or friends, they might have left me alone.

Life is filled with ups and downs. We have good times and bad. We have life and death. We have relationships and we have marriage. On one hand, a minister's marriage is like all others, and then, on the other hand, it is like no other. You might compare it to a politician's marriage because political people are under the spotlight or in a fishbowl. However, the minister's marriage is far different. You are rubbing shoulders with the same people every week and sometimes almost every day. They get to know you regardless of what you share or how much of yourself you give away. People insert themselves into your lives. The people in the church are in control of your paycheck and your housing. To some degree, it can feel as if they are in control of your entire life. It takes a tight marriage to flourish and thrive. The point is this-you can do it. Two people can make it and flourish. Keep in mind the greatest of these is love. When you love each other and love God and have a heart for each other and a heart to make it, then as an old country preacher once said, "You can jack up hell and put a stump under it."

If your ministry is killing your marriage, then start looking for another ministry. Make sure the problem is not between you and your spouse first before you start trying to move. However, if you two are good but the personality of the church is making your home life impossible, then by all means, draft the best resume you can and start circulating your name. Ask those in your ministerial leadership circles to help you to relocate to another place. For the sake of your marriage and family, it might even be better to take a secular job for a few months so that you and your family can have a break if this is what it takes to save your marriage and family.

As pastors, too often, we make the church our first priority. We love the work. We feel called to the work. We have spent our entire lives training for the work of the ministry. We have invested everything we have and everything we are into being a minister. We end up in a place in our lives where ministry is all we know, all we are called to do, and all that we feel passionate or on fire about. We are consumed by ministry. We are filled with a heart to reach people for Christ. We want to baptize people. We want our attendance at church to grow. We want the work of God that we are doing to flourish. When all this other stuff starts happening, it rips the minister's heart out. It becomes a battle to hold on to all he or she has worked toward for their entire life. Typically, the minister pours out his soul to make the ministry work and to keep the church intact and his marriage together. Often, it becomes a major juggling act. The minister becomes like the man spinning three plates on three sticks. He does it for a time, but then, eventually a plate flies off the stick, and all the others crash as well. It is heartbreaking for any of us to give everything we have to give and then realize we still haven't given enough nor is it perceived as good enough. Sadly, no matter how much we give, try to do, and try to be, we can't make it work. That is when the minister is depleted and devastated.

Hopefully, this scenario never happens to you. I do know of ministers who have spent their lives at their church and joyfully retired after 30 or more years from a beautiful fulfilling ministry. I know ministers who have moved from church to church and still retired in their sixties on their terms and felt good about their long careers in ministry.

However, if your congregation or ministry no longer wants you or you no longer want to be there, you need to be able to drive off with your spouse and family intact. After 20 years, a friend of mine resigned from his church. He said that he wanted to be with his family, and to reconnect with his wife. Many ministers, who he shared that with, nodded their heads because they understood how easy it is to lose your marriage and your family in the midst of doing your ministry.

If you are married and your wife or husband can be with you in some of what you are doing, it will work better for both of you. Making a few hospital visits together or visiting some of the shut-ins together gives you a chance to be together and do something that is typically well-received and is helpful to others. You may both get involved in helping a couple with their wedding or comforting those at a funeral. You have to be careful because if you have children, someone has to be a fixture for them. The minister and spouse cannot simply leave their kids at home, especially when they are small. Marriage and ministry are a balancing act of epic proportions.

May God bless you in your marriage and your family. May he bless you in your singleness. May you find the peace that passes all understanding and the internal joy, pleasure, and happiness that everyone deserves. Give life, love, and your ministry your very best. Try your best, do your best, be your best, and give your best. That is all anyone can do. That is what God has done for us. He gave us his best in Jesus. Jesus gave us his best every day, and yet for a very religious crowd, it was never enough, and he was not what they wanted. So, they put Jesus on a cross. However, he rose again and had newness of life. We share in that newness of life.

God is offering newness of life to everyone. He is offering newness of life to you even now. Whatever you have or are experiencing, the cross is not the end. Sometimes we feel like we have been nailed to a cross. Keep in mind there is a resurrection, and there is a glorious new life. Sometimes that new life is around the corner, in just three days. Sometimes it takes a few months or a year or two for some. However, with God and his power, life can change.

Look to him in hope and joy this day.

Chapter 5

Your Family

"Whoever claims to love God yet hates a brother or sister is a liar. For whoever does not love their brother and sister, whom they have seen, cannot love God, whom they have not seen." 1 John 4:20

"How good and pleasant it is when God's people live together in unity!" Psalm 133:1

"Honor your father and mother,' and 'love your neighbor as yourself.' Matthew 19:19

"Start children off on the way they should go,and even when they are old, they will not   turn from it." Proverbs 22:6

"Children are a heritage from the Lord, offspring a reward from him." Psalm 127:1

"Above all, love each other deeply, because love covers over a multitude of sins. [9]Offer hospitality to one another without grumbling. [10]Each of you should use whatever gift you have received to serve others, as faithful stewards of God's grace in its various forms. [11]If anyone speaks, they should do so as one who speaks the very words of God. If anyone serves, they should do so with the strength God provides, so that in all things God may be praised through Jesus Christ. To him be the glory and the power for ever and ever. Amen." 1 Peter 4: 8-11

"Be completely humble and gentle; be patient, bearing with one another in love. Make   every effort to keep the unity of the Spirit through the bond of peace." Ephesians 4:2-3

"For where two or three gather in my name, there am I with them." Matthew 18:20

"Carry each other's burdens, and in this way you will fulfill the law of Christ." Galatians 6:2

"I have no greater joy than to hear that my children are walking in the truth," 3 John 4.

"Fathers do not exasperate your children; instead, bring them up in the training and instruction of the Lord." Ephesians 6:4

"Wives, submit yourselves to your own husbands as you do to the Lord. [23]For the husband is the head of the wife as Christ is the head of the church, his body, of which he is the Savior. [24]Now as the church submits to Christ, so also wives should submit to their husbands in everything. [25]Husbands, love your wives, just as Christ loved the church and gave himself up for her [26]to make her holy, cleansing her by the washing with water through the word, [27]and to present her to himself as a radiant church, without stain or wrinkle or any other blemish, but holy and blameless. [28]In this same way, husbands ought to love their wives as their own bodies. He who loves his wife loves himself.

[29]After all, no one ever hated their own body, but they feed and care for their body, just as Christ does the church— [30]for we are members of his body. [31]"For this reason a man will leave his father and mother and be united to his wife, and the two will become one flesh." [32]This is a profound mystery—but I am talking about Christ and the church. [33]However, each one of you also must love his wife as he loves himself, and the wife must respect her husband." Ephesians 5:22-33

Your spouse and children are your priority. God should be first, family second, ministry job third. Too many ministers get ministry jobs and God confused. Love for God and commitment to God does not necessarily equate to your vocational ministry job. Your ministry job is important and may be feeding your family, but don't sacrifice your family on the altar of ministry success. I know that I have already said this, but it is important.

If you spend all your time during the week in church meetings, church outreach, church get-togethers, multiple prayer services, multiple worship services, and whatever else, you'll not have time for your spouse and children. The childhood and teenage years will be your only real time with them. When your children leave home for school, work, or the military, you won't see them or spend much time with them. You'll be fortunate if you see them much at all. When they marry and have their own children, they'll be busy spending time with their children and spouse and living their lives and careers. They won't have a lot of time for you. If you want to spend time with your children, then do it while they are at home. Look for every opportunity you can find to spend time with them. Play with them, work with them, help them, mentor them, teach them, and love on them. If you don't, the day will come when you wish you had. You can't turn back the clock and get a second opportunity to spend time with your family. Do it today.

Duty calls, and you must earn your pay. Church leadership places a lot of demands on ministers. They want them to have office hours, be at the evening activities, visit all the sick and shut-ins, win the lost people, and preach perfectly. You can't do all of the above, all the time without neglecting your family.

You need to be as tight with your spouse and children as the ring on your finger. If the ministry is making your family miserable, then you need to take a break and do something else. You might consider taking a smaller ministry, or a different ministry job, or even doing a different kind of work for a while. There is no shame in this. Too many ministers hold on to jobs for financial security, recognition, status, or the sheer love of the position. Often, ministers hold on to their ministry jobs because they worry about what others might think. They think there is shame in taking a break to do something else. If you live your life based on what others think, you'll never live your own life. You'll never be happy, and neither will your family.

I understand "calling." I know what it means to be "called" of God to preach, teach, evangelize, serve, and lead in ministry. God doesn't call you to destroy your children or your family while you fulfill your call.

Every job is tough when you are committed to doing and giving your best. For over 30 years, my father was an underground coal miner. I saw him on some Saturdays and a little bit on Sundays. He took a two-week vacation in the summer. He never had the time to spend with our family like was afforded me in pastoral ministries. While I was a pastor, I would say that our family almost always ate dinner together. It might have been at a fast-food restaurant or a microwave pizza, but we had dinner together almost always. Usually, the average minister will be able to fit in a child's ballgame, take their children to their next event, and be involved in what their children are doing. Often, ministers will be able to tweak their schedules to be a part of what is going on at home.

One pastor friend, who I admire, told his congregation that Tuesday was his day off, and he wasn't kidding. On Tuesday, he and his wife could not be found. He didn't go to the funeral home, do funerals, or anything ministerial on Tuesday. It seems that funeral directors don't care about the minister's day off. They will schedule a funeral to suit everybody else's schedule, especially theirs. My friend held to his position about not doing anything on Tuesday, everybody eventually got the message, and he had a real day off. You have to do this at the beginning and not budge. Once you give in, a few times, then everyone knows that you are wishy-washy about it, and you'll never have a real day off.

Keep your focus on your ministry job. You don't need to belong to every community organization in town. If you spend all your time volunteering for all the civic organizations, then you will be depleting your resources from your real job and family. Don't get caught up in money-making schemes and allow people to use you. When someone wants to get you in their network of trying to make a dollar, the angle is to help them and not you. They'll use you to benefit themselves. They like to be able to pitch your name to the people who are involved in their money-making projects. Do not do it. Don't let others involve you in their little money-making projects. Every year there is a newnetwork marketing scheme that somebody in your church or community will get involved in doing. They will try to get the ministers involved because of their influence and name recognition. Again, don't do it. They'll only use you. You will not benefit from this drain on your life and time.

It is fine for you to be ambitious and creative if you need to make some money. Many ministers are bi-vocational. Many are because they have to be, and many are because they want to be. My dad always told me to get a good job and preach on the side. Most of us squirm a little when we hear that philosophy of preaching on the side. It's as if it doesn't have much of a priority in our lives. It might have a greater priority if you were able to go to the pulpit or the church without so much strain, worry, and fear that some ministers, who have full-time church or ministry jobs, often carry.

There is something about being a tentmaker as was the Apostle Paul, or helping to pay your own way. Another friend of mine pastored a church for over 30 years. That church averaged over

500 people in attendance every Sunday. He took a little money for expenses and had a full-time staff. He preached, attended a couple of meetings a week, and visited some. He was busy. I'm not sure how much time he had for his family. I can't imagine that he had a lot of time, but he seemed to be very happy in his life and ministry. Consider this verse from the Apostle Paul in Second Thessalonians 3:8, "nor did we eat anyone's food without paying for it. On the contrary, we worked night and day, laboring and toiling so that we would not be a burden to any of you." That, of course, is not easy. That is also why many ministers prefer a full-time, church-supported ministry so they can focus on doing their ministry and have some family life.

Don't let your denomination take all your time. Denominations are desperate for more money. They want to keep money coming from your church. They want to put you on committees in your denomination to make you feel important. It's all about keeping the money coming from your church. It's not that they always think you are great. They want to use you to build up their state or national headquarters.

In November 1991, I became President of the Kentucky Baptist Convention. I was the youngest person ever elected to the job and the youngest person ever elected by acclamation. I had already served as the President of the state Pastor's Conference in 1990. During this same period, Karen was diagnosed with multiple sclerosis.

Multiple sclerosis is an insidious disease that brought about rapid declining health for Karen during this time. One of the last times she played the piano was at the state convention meeting that I presided over in November of 1992.

The year I served, and the year or two after I served as state convention President, she was still able to drive and do most of life on her own. Looking back, I wish I had tossed even the thought of denominational service to the side, at least for that time. Often, when we are young, we think everything has to be "now." It doesn't have to be now. It can be later, and if it doesn't happen later then, that's okay. A job like a denominational state convention President takes a lot of time away from your family and your real ministry job that pays the bills. Plus, it doesn't pay any money. It's strictly a volunteer service. It is a great service for an older minister whose family is grown. He and or she and the spouse can do it together later in life. I don't think it's a great job for a younger minister. You have to think about this and make your decisions. My wife's overwhelming illness has greatly colored my perspective on all of this. If she had not become so ill, it might have been just a flash in the pan year in my life, never to be thought about again.

Too often, we grab for the brass ring. We envision a position, a job, or an opportunity that we think would be gratifying. We often think that such a place of service, position, or appointment might enhance our career or propel us to more and greater opportunities. Sometimes it does, and sometimes we are disappointed that it's not what we thought it would be.

We are back again to family. Keep in mind that it's God, family, and then your real job that pays the bills. You can have little hobbies. Mine has mostly been writing throughout my life. You may play golf, exercise, enjoy sports, garden, work on cars, or whatever. Every minister needs an outlet. It's healthy to be able to get your mind off other things. It is also healthy to not have so many hobbies that you don't have time to do your real job and be connected to your family. It's a job of balancing all of this that you and God have to figure out. No one else can figure it out for you. Your spouse and children may help you figure it out. Talk to them about all this. Include them in what is going on. Do some family talking and planning. Get their ideas about your schedule. Work together. Everybody in the family has to give and take some. At least if you are talking about it, then you are talking. The family must keep talking, walking, and working together.

I could never write enough about how great my family was during my many years of pastoral ministry. We had a couple of years where we moved, moved again, and moved again, it seemed. One year my two sons were in three different schools as we were trying to find a way to get settled in Indiana. The toll of beginning a new ministry at a church in Southern, Indiana, my wife's increasing debilitation due to multiple sclerosis, and trying to fit life and ministry together was challenging. My two sons hung tight. Our church grew by about 400%. We built a magnificent facility and had a great ministry with great numbers, finances, and fellowship. The church was great and hung tight during most of my 10-year ministry until my sons' mother passed away. We all cried most every day and struggled with her deteriorating health and extreme health challenges. In the middle of all this despair and pain, our church prayed and did very well. Our family prayed a lot, stressed a lot, hurt a lot, and lived mostly in a survival mode for many years. It wasn't fun. It's was a form of hell in many ways. God took care of us, and we were able to pay the bills, eat, and keep our family intact and suffer together through a difficult time.

My sons' mother passed away in November 2002. They were 17 and 20 years old at the time. Karen was 49 when she passed after fighting the MS battle for 12 years. I have to stop here to cry because these last two sentences tear me to shreds.

I'll wrap up this chapter by saying when your ministry service is over, it will be you and your spouse and your family that is left. The church ministry is our family in many ways while we are there, but it's not when we leave. Most of the time, after you leave a church ministry, it's like a death, or maybe even a divorce. The new minister who comes doesn't even want you around. Your old congregation doesn't want you hanging around influencing whatever they now want to do. If you move on to another church field of service, they often will resent you for leaving them for greener pastures. So, when you resign or retire to go somewhere else, all those years and all the attention you gave those people are over and done. What you have left are your spouse and your children and family connections. Therefore, take good care of these people because they are the ones who are with you now and will be with you, hopefully, when your tenure of ministry service is complete. Nurture them and keep them close, every day of your ministry, so that your family will remain intact when your ministry is finished.

Chapter 6

Your Home and Church Parsonage

The Bible says, "Do not muzzle an ox while it is treading out the grain," and "The worker deserves his wages." 1 Timothy 5:18

"The elders who direct the affairs of the church well are worthy of double honor,especially those whose work is preaching and teaching," 1 Timothy 5:17

"This is my defense to those who sit in judgment on me. [4]Don't we have the right to food and drink? [5]Don't we have the right to take a believing wife along with us, as do the other apostles and the Lord's brothers and Cephas? [6]Or is it only I and Barnabas who lack the right to not work for a living? 1 Corinthians 9: 3-6

"Who serves as a soldier at his own expense? Who plants a vineyard and does not eat its grapes? Who tends a flock and does not drink the milk?" 1 Corinthians 9:7

"If we have sown spiritual seed among you, is it too much if we reap a material harvest from you? [12]If others have this right of support from you, shouldn't we have it all the more?But we did not use this right. On the contrary, we put up with anything rather than hinder the gospel of Christ. [13]Don't you know that those who serve in the temple get their food from the temple, and that those who serve at the altar share in what is offered on the altar? 1 Corinthians 9: 11-13

When I moved out of the parsonage, I felt like I had moved out of prison-almost. I am grateful for every church-owned home, and I am grateful for every opportunity I had to move out of them.

My first parsonage was while serving as pastor of the Forks of Elkhorn Baptist Church, Ducker's Station, Midway, Kentucky. The parsonage was an old white house with a recently remodeled upstairs that was nice, but the basement was dungeon-like. One side of the basement had been remodeled, with an outside entrance, so that the youth group of the church had a place to meet. That was always a bit creepy because the outside door was never locked. Anybody could be in the youth room, which was directly under the bedroom where my wife and I slept.

The laundry room was also in the basement. To this day, Forks of Elkhorn Baptist Church sits in open horse country. The church has a mega-sized facility, worship center, family life recreational center, and much more. However, they are smack dab in the middle of bluegrass farming country, which happens to be one of the most beautiful places in the world. At this writing, the old church where I served and the old white parsonage still stand and are in use.

Being in such a country setting with an old house and a basement, not even close to being sealed tight, presented lots of opportunities for critters.

The first time that Karen barreled up the basement steps in fear and trembling because she had seen a large rat, I could hardly believe it. After I went down and saw what looked like a rat, the size of a rabbit, scurrying around in the back of the basement, trying to stay out of my way, but not very afraid of me, I believed.

On more than one occasion, we saw not one but often two or three rats scurrying through this basement. When we moved to this church field, we had left a nice, suburban apartment in Trotwood/Dayton, Ohio. The apartment was small, but we didn't have mice and rats. Karen had left her parent's home in Englewood, Ohio, where their laundry room was in the basement, but it was a new house. The basement was newly poured, and the house was very tight. This basement laundry room setting was a new adventure for us in washing clothes. The days of going down in the basement barefoot were over. We always donned a pair of shoes and jeans as we went down to face the wild.

Overall the parsonage we lived in upstairs was clean. We had two good bedrooms on the main floor, a living room, a dining room, and an ample sized kitchen. Upstairs was a room we turned into a television room. On one end of that room, there was a study room, which was great for me. Some of my first writing was done in this room.

The old white house was not very insulated, if at all. The heat was unbearable as Kentucky's summer days can settle into the nineties and occasionally hit 100 degrees. To say that we were roasting in that house would be an understatement. Small fans and open windows after a while do not bring any relief from that kind of oppressive heat.

I approached the leaders of the church about air conditioning the parsonage, and they had about as much interest in putting air conditioning in the house as they did in riding a pontoon boat to China-none. One of the leaders of the church, who had gotten control of almost all the decisions about maintaining the church buildings and property, told me from the start that he was against air conditioning the parsonage. Obviously, it would cost money. The church was still a small church averaging about 50 people, and funds were tight. On a quick side note here, the church did grow. In one year, we baptized more than had been baptized the previous five years, and our attendance became more like 80 to 100 each week, which was very good for this country church. Karen and I bought a used window unit air conditioner for our bedroom, and we survived the situation. Further, I do not want to come off here as ungrateful or unappreciative. We appreciated the house and a place to live.

Some of the sweetest dearest people I have ever known and know to this day were in the Forks of Elkhorn Baptist Church. To this day, some of my best friends still attend this church. This church today has the best of everything in facilities, outreach, worship, and plenty of air conditioning.

What I experienced at this church is typical of small churches that will put a pastor into a parsonage and count it as part of his salary. The church people are usually very proud of their parsonage.

Since our church grew with baptisms, lots of young families, and increased giving, it didn't take long for another church to extend an invitation to me to serve as their pastor. Stamping Ground Baptist Church, in Stamping Ground, Kentucky, was close to Georgetown. In 1980 Stamping Ground had one of the prettiest church facilities in Central, Kentucky. It had been completely rebuilt, following the 1974 tornado that demolished the community and all the churches. The facility the church built was simply gorgeous. For a young 24-year-old preacher, the pulpit, fancy stained-glass windows, the sanctuary, pastor's office, and more provided an incredible place to study, preach sermons and do the Lord's work. The congregation, like most rural congregations, was smaller than the Forks of Elkhorn Church that I had left. Stamping Ground was only averaging about 40 people and would struggle to pay me $1,200 a month plus provide us with a parsonage.

The parsonage at that time was a nice, large, somewhat modern looking house for that era. The poured concrete garage would park two cars easily. Inside this garage was also the washer and dryer that required going down the steps to do laundry but was much brighter, cleaner, and suitable than the parsonage we had left. It was not what we would have chosen in a house, but when you move into a church parsonage, you take what they have to offer you.

Stamping Ground's parsonage, like Forks of Elkhorn Church, did not have air conditioning. In the winter, it was expensive to heat. The source of heat was a big propane tank that sat outside the house, which could easily cost a couple of thousand dollars to fill. One filling of that tank never made it through the winter, so normally, around the end of February or early March, it would require another half-filling. This type of expense for heat was a budget breaker. The church did not and would not cover the expense of heating their parsonage. Sadly, they had a nice house but couldn't afford to cover the heating expense.

The church eventually bought a wood-burning stove. They spent about $600 on a wood-burning insert that fit into the fireplace that was in the living room. The house was so drafty in the winter that I was delighted to have a way to at least warm most of the house. Yet, the church didn't buy the wood. My new hobby became buying wood that I would often have to split with an ax so that it would fit into the stove. My mom and dad had given up coal/wood-burning stoves when I was a child. We had become accustomed to a natural gas burning furnace that was in the middle of our house. Karen had never lived in a house with a wood-burning stove, so this was new to us. Splitting wood was good exercise, and it got me outdoors in some brisk air, which was enjoyable.

Stamping Ground had the same problem with air conditioning. The house was large, and they were not interested in spending the money to install central air conditioning. We ended up buying a window unit for the dining room and a window unit for the bedroom, and thus, we simply had to make do.

Stamping Ground Baptist Church tripled in attendance and at least doubled in our giving. We had 40 people in this very rural community to join the church in the first few months we were there. On Sunday morning, the church was full most of the time and very well attended on Sunday nights. After not quite three years, First Baptist Church, Highland Heights, Kentucky, came to see me.

Highland Heights is the home of Northern Kentucky University and is a progressive community. A church located close to a growing university was appealing. They were already averaging over 200 in attendance, and Campbell County was exploding in population. One problem they had was they did not have a parsonage. They didn't particularly want a parsonage. They wanted the preacher to own his own home, and I was all for that as well.

The local Baptist Director of Missions wanted to retire and sell his house. He wanted to sell on a land contract and was willing to sell the house without one penny of down payment. He had a very well-built house that he had never painted or done upkeep to, but they were minor things that we could fix.

The Director of Missions saw selling his house on a land contract to the right buyer as retirement income for him. We would pay $800 a month for 20 years at a 10% interest rate. This was at a time when 10% was a good deal on interest rates. The church even increased their salary package a bit to help us get into the house, and the move to Northern, Kentucky, was in progress.

We received a strong vote by the Highland Heights church and soon were moving into our very own home. We were moving out of a parsonage and into a place we could call our own home To say we were excited is an understatement.

We were fortunate that a nice house, with such a deal, came along. Land contracts can be a great way to purchase a house. Often, they don't require a large down payment, and the owner, who is the seller, is typically trying to find a way to unload his property and may even make other considerations that make buying the house very attractive. Keep in mind if you don't make your payments, the house goes back to the owner. Typically, if you get 60 days behind, the contract will state that you are to vacate the premises and surrender the house back to the owner. Land contracts read differently, and the seller and the buyer can set up any terms they want.

Being in our own home was a secure feeling. We had central heat and air conditioning. We could paint our house any color we wanted. We could trim our bushes or choose whatever color carpet we wanted, and we did. The freedom of living in our own house was, in many ways, like being released from bondage.

Apartment living is almost as bad. Landlords and apartment managers keep tenants under constant surveillance. We also had personal experiences with apartments, and they felt very restraining to our lifestyles. You don't just paint a rented apartment. Some places don't want pets. There are lots of rules that come with apartment living.

The only problem with owning your own house is that you pay for everything. You pay all your utilities. You pay to replace your roof when it needs replacing. You pay to replace your furnace if it goes out. You pay the property taxes and all upkeep. For ministers, this still has an upside as ordained ministers have been privileged to designate their house payment and house expenses as ministerial house expenses. The Internal Revenue Service in the United States has exempted this portion of the minister's salary from federal income tax, which has provided extra cash for the minister. The minister still has to pay the social security part of the tax. That can end up being a lot of money that the minister pays quarterly or gets stuck with a large tax payment in April of each year.

There is a cost to freedom. Freedom is never cheap or easy. Living in your own house is almost always better than living in a church-owned house or anybody else's house. There are certain situations where it works out great. Ministers almost always look at living in a parsonage for a brief period. The hope is that it works well for a short period. Often, many ministers live in a church-owned house until they retire and then have no place to go. The church counts the parsonage as part of the pastor's salary as free rent, but they don't pay the minister enough to save any money. I know many pastors who moved out of nice parsonages into apartments, trailers, or government-subsidized housing at their retirement. Occasionally, I have heard of pastors who were paid enough to save enough money to buy their own home, but it's not the norm.

The church at Highland Heights was a great ministry with all the numbers going in the right direction. Our attendance continued to grow. I baptized a lot of people, plus we had a lot of other people who moved their membership from other churches to Highland Heights. I do not remember the total number of additions for the three years that I was at the church, but they were good. The financial offerings grew, and we had a sweet spirit of fellowship and harmony in the church.

During my ministry at Highland Heights, I completed my Doctor of Ministry degree with The Lexington Theological Seminary, Lexington, Kentucky. With a robust church, a new earned doctorate and wearing braces to correct my teeth, I was still only 29 years old when First Baptist Church, Pikeville, Kentucky, started calling me.

First Baptist Church Pikeville is in the far corner of central Eastern, Kentucky. Geographically, they are the largest county east of the Mississippi River. In 1984 they were in the middle of the biggest coal boom ever seen in Eastern, Kentucky. People were everywhere, and businesses were booming. Coal operators, bankers, real estate brokers, lawyers, and doctors were all getting rich. Houses in the area were outrageously expensive. A single lot, in one subdivision in the city of Pikeville, was listed at over $100,000. That's still a lot of money to pay for a lot, but in 1984, it was crazy expensive for a town of 5500 people in the middle of Appalachia.

First Baptist Pikeville had a fairly nice parsonage in one of the better subdivisions in the county. The house needed some work but overall had been well maintained. The bathroomsin the house were outdated.

During my eight and half years as their pastor, the church never considered updating them. I moved Karen and our first son Jared to Pikeville in July 1984. When I told the Highland Heights church that I had accepted a call to Pikeville, Kentucky, one of my deacons, who was and is a friend, asked, "Have you lost your mind?"

I wanted to go to Pikeville for several reasons. I was raised about an hour from Pikeville, Kentucky and my parents were still alive and very active at that time. I had numerous other family members in nearby Martin County.

In 1984, Pikeville was a dead church averaging, on a great day, maybe 200 but often well below 200 in attendance. At that time, the church was still one of the largest churches in East, Kentucky.

I felt like my ministry opportunities would be greater in Pikeville. The main question with all ministerial moves is, "Did God call you?" God was definitely in the call as I saw the fields white unto harvest. Keep in mind a lot goes into a call to another church. God will call us if we want to go and if we are willing to go and serve him. Any ole place will do when it comes to the Lord's work. I could have stayed in Highland Heights. Looking back, I would have been better off in many ways to have stayed there, but it's a waste to look back. Nothing is accomplished by looking back. We can remember and try to learn from our mistakes or be nostalgic about the past, but life is lived going forward.

Karen, Jared, and I moved into the parsonage of the First Baptist Church, Pikeville, to start our new lives in East, Kentucky. I had decided to rent my house in Northern, Kentucky, which was tough from four hours away. I didn't have any trouble finding someone to rent it, but the rent check was normally late. That was tough since I still had a payment to make every month. Within six months, I decided to sell the house. It sold rather quickly, and we pocketed $10,000 of profit on the house. Remember, I paid nothing down on the house. We lived in the house for about three years and came out with some cash. That's not always easy to do but, the house was in a nice suburb in Cold Spring, Kentucky, and Northern, Kentucky has had a good economy and opportunities for many years.

Having free rent took a lot of the pressure off, but in the end, the financial pressure "rains" down on your head when it's time to move. You have to have enough money saved to buy or put down on a house. For most pastors, when you move, that's tough.

I have looked back and thought that if I had stayed in Highland Heights and paid on that $80,000 mortgage, I would have had a house paid for by the time I was 46 years old and probably would have paid it off sooner. Hindsight is always better than foresight.

When we left Pikeville, there were four of us because my second son Zachary had been born in October 1985. We lived in Pikeville for over eight years. Karen worked part-time in the schools, and we had tried to save money knowing that the day would come. We moved to Louisa, Kentucky, where we bought a house. We had saved enough for a down payment. We lived in that house for about 18 months before I accepted a call to Gateway Baptist Church, Newburgh, Indiana, and we put the house in Louisa up for sale. We moved into a very small, two-bedroom apartment in Evansville, Indiana, and lived in that apartment for a year. From the sale of the Louisa house, I ended up with what I needed, to the penny, for us to buy a house in Newburgh, Indiana.

The point here to all this unending information is to urge you and encourage you to think about investing in your own house. Everyone needs a place to live. Apartment dwelling seems to be on the rise today, but I think it's because many people have poor credit and can't get into houses or simply do not have enough money to put down on a house. Often, poor credit keeps people out of apartments.

In our area of Southern, Indiana, there are two-and one-bedroom apartments everywhere to rent. Some are cheaper than others and even include the cost of utilities. We have a number of apartments reasonably priced to the 55 and over age community. They look very nice. Some of them even have an attached garage, two bathrooms, and spacious dining and living rooms. There is an ongoing waiting list of seniors wanting to rent these apartments. They are building new ones every time they can come up with a spare acre of land. For the minister who has lived in a parsonage his entire life, these types of apartments are lifesavers. A couple moving out of a parsonage at 65 or 70 years old are very unlikely to feel like taking on a 20-year mortgage.

However, one of my friends did just that. He retired at 65 at a church in Northern, Kentucky, moved to Louisville, bought a house in St. Matthews, lived in it for 20 years, and paid it off. He and his wife lived close to the St. Matthews Mall, where they went walking almost every day for exercise. At about age 85, they sold their home and moved into a senior adult assisted living facility owned by a church in Louisville. The sale of the house gave them the cash they needed for the next eight or so years in which they both lived comfortably in their assisted living quarters.

Chapter 7

Why should you buy a house?

You need a place to live. It's simple. When you own a house, the only way you can lose it is if you don't make your monthly payment or you don't pay your property taxes. Also, pay your taxes to the Internal Revenue Service if you live in the United States because if you don't, they will get involved in your income and the property that you own. That is another reason some people live in apartments. Taxes become an issue, and they have to give up their home because they did not or could not pay their taxes. One plus of apartment living is avoiding the property tax. However, local and state governments find ways to tax everything, so there may be taxes associated with apartment living where you live.

When it's your house, you can do what you want to do. You can paint it any color, have pets or not and make it your world in which you live. It always takes money. Updating a bathroom will cost you in the thousands. A new roof will cost thousands, so there is a price to owning your own home. People enjoy this for a long time, and especially when you are raising a family and need the space. Often people get to a place where they are more interested in playing golf, fishing, and traveling. Spending all their time keeping up a lot of property becomes less interesting. When this happens, and you have been paying on your house for 15 or 20 years, you will have equity. You can sell your house and have some cash to make whatever transition you want to make. Perhaps to a smaller place, or maybe to rent a place, in another state, but you have some options.

When you rent your whole life or have lived in a church-owned house, and you haven't saved a lot of money, then you have no equity. You have nothing to sell to obtain extra cash that you would need through the selling of your house.

There is nothing wrong with renting. Keep in mind that when you rent, you will always have rent to pay. You aren't building equity unless you can save money each month in some kind of savings account. When you rent, there are landlords, community regulations, and at some point, rent usually goes up.

When you are making house payments, there is a chance you will always make a house payment. If you buy a house when you are 65 and finance it for 20 years, you might pay it off, and you might not. If the payment on your house is not any more, or much more than a rental payment would be, you may not care. However, the house will be yours. When you die, your surviving spouse will hopefully have someplace to live, or your surviving family can sell it and divide the equity.

Making house payments is better than living in a church-owned home. If the congregation or leadership pushes you out of your job, you can at least go back to "your" house. When you are in a parsonage, they want you out of the house as soon as possible. Small town churches not only count on you moving out of the parsonage, but they count on you having to move to another town to find work. They typically don't want the minister they have terminated staying in town in fear that you will start another church or in fear that another local congregation might hire you. That could lend to the possibility that some of the church members would follow you to another local ministry. When you own your own house, you can go back to your house and start looking for another ministry or at least another job to help you pay your bills and financially survive.

Buying a house depends on a lot of variables. Normally, you have to have some money to make a down payment. Often this is 20% of the house's selling price. Sometimes you can arrange to get in for less than 20% down which may mean you can't afford to buy the house. You have to have the income to make the payment. You might stretch it out to 30 years. If you are under 60, you have a chance of living to be 90, if you are healthy. Why pay 30 years on a mortgage? Pay it off in 15 to 20 years and be done with it. The cost of paying for a house in 15 to 20 years will save you tens of thousands of dollars in comparison to a 30-year loan.

Some seniors today are talking about buying property and financing it for a long time knowing that they will never live to pay it off, and of course, they don't care. One man in our town was in his nineties and not in great health when he bought a new car on a seven-year loan. He enjoyed it for a couple of years, and when he died, his daughter took it back and handed the keys over to the dealership.

Finally, look for deals. Some people are willing to sell their house on a land contract. Normally, they will accept a smaller down payment than a bank or finance company might require. Make sure your attorney looks over any papers you sign and that it's a fair contract. You pay the seller a specified amount for an agreed-upon term. Keep copies of every check you write in this kind of a deal. Make sure that the person you are buying it from has a clear title and that they are not selling you something that they have second mortgaged or have liens on. Get your attorney involved in this kind of purchase.

There are lots of houses for sale where people are desperate to get rid of them. There are cases where people overbought, have lost their jobs, are going through bankruptcy or divorce or illness, and all kinds of terrible things. They have to sell, and somebody will buy what they are selling. Situations like these might present a good opportunity for you to get into a house.

Often, banks have property that people couldn't make payments for, and they are quite willing to sell for a more reasonable price. They probably have already made a lot of money off the house from the previous mortgage.

There could be a family member you could buy a house from. It could be that someone in your family can't afford to give you a house outright but would be happy to give you a good deal on the house. For example, not having a real estate agent involved in the sale can help reduce the price by thousands of dollars. Someone in your family might be willing to let their house go to you for several thousands of dollars less so that they can go ahead and get rid of it. Plus, they know they are helping you out at the same time. You never know until you ask around.

Be creative and be thinking about this because having a place to live is vitally important. We are seeing a growing epidemic of homelessness around the world. This is tragic. How sad it is when a minister of God has served a congregation or several congregations his/her entire life, and essentially, they have no place to call their own when the churches they have served no longer have any use for them. There are options. There are trailers that are typically cheaper to get into, and they are building them better all the time. There is senior adult housing, old houses that require some fixing up, and on and on. Renting a place, or whatever direction you can go, is better than being homeless.

You have to think about this. I know many ministers live with the philosophy "I'm not going to worry about it, God will take care of me." God will take care of you by helping you take care of yourself. Look to God in prayer. Ask him for wisdom. Ask him for guidance. Ask him to empower you, and yes, God will help you. Hopefully, God is helping you through what you are reading at this moment. Take care of yourself and your family. Secure a place to live. When your church or place of ministry is finished with you, they will give you a month or two to get out of their house so they can move the next minister in. They will be done with you.

The story is told of a man trying to survive a flood. He climbed on the roof of his house, and another man came by in a boat and offered him a ride, but the man on the roof said, "God will take care of me." Another man came by in a second boat and offered the man on the roof, now ankle-deep in water, a ride. The man on the roof said, "No, God will take care of me." Finally, the water was waist-deep on the man. He was about to be washed away when a helicopter appeared and tried to save him, but the man refused to be airlifted as he exclaimed to the rescue team, "No, God will save me." A few minutes later, the man drowned and stood before God. He looked at God and said, "Why didn't you save me?" God replied, "I sent you two boats and a helicopter."

Sometimes ministers don't get the two boats and a helicopter. However, hopefully, common sense, some hard work, and sacrifice will make it possible for you to have a secure and safe dwelling place for you and your family.

Chapter 8

Save Money for Retirement

"But remember the LORD your God, for it is he who gives you the ability to produce wealth, and so confirms his covenant, which he swore to your ancestors, as it is today," Deuteronomy 8:18

"A wise man thinks ahead; a fool doesn't, and even brags about it!" Proverbs 13:16

"The wise store up choice food and olive oil, but fools gulp theirs down." Proverbs 21:20

"Dishonest money dwindles away, but he who gathers money little by little makes it grow." Proverbs 13:11

"For it is just like a man about to go on a journey, who called his own slaves and entrusted his possessions to them. To one he gave five talents, to another, two, and to another, one, each according to his own ability; and he went on his journey. Immediately the one who had received the five talents went and traded with them and gained five more talents. In the same manner the one who had received the two talents gained two more. But he who received the one talent went away and dug a hole in the ground and hid his master's money. Now after a long time the master of those slaves came and settled accounts with them. The one who had received the five talents came up and brought five more talents, saying, 'Master, you entrusted five talents to me. See, I have gained five more talents.' His master said to him, 'Well done, good and faithful slave You were faithful with a few things, I will put you in charge of many things; enter into the joy of your master.' Also, the one who had received the two talents came up and said, 'Master, you entrusted two talents to me. See, I have gained two more talents.' His master said to him, 'Well done, good and faithful slave. You were faithful with a few things; I will put you in charge of many things; enter into the joy of your master.' And the one also who had received the one talent came up and said, 'Master, I knew you to be a hard man, reaping where you did not sow and gathering where you scattered no seed. And I was afraid and went away and hid your talent in the ground. See, you have what is yours.' But his master answered and said to him, 'You wicked, lazy slave, you knew that I reap where I did not sow and gather where I scattered no seed. 'Then you ought to have put my money in the bank, and on my arrival, I would have received my money back with interest. Therefore, take away the talent from him, and give it to the one who has the ten talents.' For to everyone who has, more shall be given, and he will have an abundance; but from the one who does not have, even what he does have shall be taken away. Throw out the worthless slave into the outer darkness; in that place there will be weeping and gnashing of teeth." Matthew 25: 14-30

"For which of you, intending to build a tower, does not sit down first and count the cost, whether he has enough to finish it—lest, after he has laid the foundation, and is not able to finish, all who see it begin to mock him, saying 'This man began to build and was not able to finish'?" Luke 14: 28-30

"Go to the ant, you sluggard; consider its ways and be wise! It has no commander, no overseer or ruler, yet it stores its provisions in summer and gathers its food at harvest." Proverbs 6: 6-8

"Plans fail for lack of counsel, but with many advisers they succeed." Proverbs 15:22

"In their hearts humans plan their course, but the LORD establishes their steps." Proverbs 16:9

"Be diligent to know the state of your flocks and attend to your herds." Proverbs 27:23

"The plans of the diligent lead to profit as surely as haste leads to poverty. "Proverbs 21:5

"Let Pharaoh appoint commissioners over the land to take a fifth of the harvest of Egypt during the seven years of abundance. They should collect all the food of these good years that are coming and store up the grain under the authority of Pharaoh, to be kept in the cities for food. This food should be held in reserve for the country, to be used during the seven years of famine that will come upon Egypt, so that the country may not be ruined by the famine." Genesis 41: 34-36

"On the first day of every week, each one of you should set aside a sum of money in keeping with your income, saving it up, so that when I come no collections will have to be made." 1 Corinthians 16:2

"The prudent see danger and take refuge, but the simple keep going and pay the penalty." Proverbs 27:12

"Four things on earth are small, yet they are extremely wise: Ants are creatures of little strength, yet they store up their food in the summer; Proverbs 30:24-25

Too many ministers arrive at retirement age without any money. Clergy members shouldn't talk about money, right? Wrong. You had better think about money, teach others about money, work to earn a respectable wage, and have a systematic savings plan. If you don't, you will regret it especially, between the age of 65 and the day you die.

For some reason, some ministers think they aren't supposed to spend time planning their retirement and trying to build a savings account for their old age. They believe they will pastor a church forever. They think some church or ministry is going to keep them up in a house and with an allowance for the rest of their lives. That's not how it will turn out for you.

When I was 29 years old, a former church member said, "Don't worry about retirement Glenn, when you are old, you will just keep on preaching." I certainly want to preach as I have the opportunity, but I don't want to have to preach just to keep food on the table.

My dad was an underground coal miner for over 30 years. I realize that I refer to this more than once. At the age of 55, he was tired and done with being an underground coal miner, and so he retired. He did not retire with a big check. His miner's pension was small and certainly not enough to live on. He eventually began to collect Social Security and other miner's benefits. He and my mother owned their own home and some land they gardened and farmed. Somehow, they raised five kids, and he and my mother managed to make it okay in their retirement years. They didn't have a lot of extra money, but they ate, dressed, and occasionally bought a car and were able to go to the doctor. Also, and this is a big one, they never worked at another job after my dad retired. They were able to manage on what they had coming in. My father made a little bit on his farming, but that only lasted a few years after his retirement.

It seems that older people and ministers who have to work in their retirement years are prevalent around the world. I see this every day in the United States. We have a Social Security system that provides retirement income to people once they become a certain age. The age used to be 65. Then, the age was raised to 67. The deal with Social Security is that you receive a better check if you pay more into the Social Security fund. If you wait until you are 70 years old to begin collecting the Social Security check, you will collect more. These figures are always changing. Who knows what it will be one year from today or especially

20 years from today. Many Americans begin collecting Social Security at the age of 62, and the payout is much smaller. Many Americans, who I know personally, are collecting much smaller checks than these amounts that I have referenced. At the age of 73, one man said his monthly Social Security check is $1,100 a month. A relative of mine says that his check is about $1,400 a month. My deceased wife collected Social Security disability of only $550 a month. I have another family member who is collecting over $2200 a month, and another one collecting a little more than that in Social Security disability. Some people collect over $3,000 a month.

The payout of Social Security depends on what you put into the fund, and most people don't get very excited about paying a lot of Social Security taxes. For the millions of Americans who are now receiving small Social Security disability checks, those amounts are based on how much they were making, at the time, they were employed. If they were making a lot of money, paying a lot into the system and became hurt or sick, and then became approved to collect disability, their check was based on what they would have collected at retirement age. Their monthly check was based on how many years they paid into Social Security and how much they were paying into the system up until the time of their disability.

Retired Americans are dependent on Social Security for their livelihood. There is a very small percentage of our American citizens who could survive without their monthly Social Security checks. Some Americans have government pensions because they worked for their state or federal government, have schoolteacher retirements, or worked for the railroad. These pensions may not include a Social Security retirement but are normally much more than the average Social Security check. People who have retired from working for the United States post office receive a government pension but not a Social Security pension. However, the pensions I have heard about are typically much more than Social Security checks.

Pay into Social Security. I'm already receiving letters telling me that a few years down the road that our federal government will not have enough money to cover all the payments that will be owed to America's citizens. A cut of what we are supposed to be due is already being promised. This is very disconcerting for all of us who are figuring the Social Security dollar amount into our annual budget of living expenses. Still, I must declare and cry out to you to pay Social Security taxes and pay as much as you can. The more you pay into the system the more you will collect when you are 67 years old.

Most ministers get a bad deal from their churches when it comes to how the church handles their salaries. For quite some time, most churches never gave their ministers 1099s and definitely not W-2s for tax reporting. Some ministers reported very little to the Internal Revenue Service of the United States and got by with reporting very little. Ministers did this for more than one reason and mostly because they could not come up with $5,000 to $10,000 at the end of the year to pay their taxes. So, by reporting a low salary, they might get by with paying only a few hundred dollars to the Internal Revenue Service. Ministers are also allowed to use mileage deductions which always end up in the thousands of miles. That can be a big deduction and saves a minister a lot of money. Also, for any housing expenses, such as a house payment, the minister receives a tax break on income tax. That saves the minister money on paying taxes. The minister still has to pay Social Security taxes on the housing allowance. The bottom line here is that each year the average minister is getting their earned salary figure as low as they can to report to the Internal Revenue Service, which means they are paying a minimal amount in Social Security taxes. That comes back to haunt the minister in old age because it will mean a minimal Social Security check in retirement years.

Years ago, a dear friend, who is now with the Lord, told me that he had opted out of Social Security. In our country, the Internal Revenue Service will let a young minister opt-out of paying into Social Security if they state religious objections or reasons for not paying into the fund. That has to be done as a young adult and is not allowed later on for ministers. He is the only one I know of personally who opted out. I saw it become crushingly sad for him. He served as an Associate Minister at a large church and received a nice salary. He did pay into his denomination's retirement plan and had saved some money that way. Yet when he retired, his monthly annuity check from his denomination, was still not as much as his Social Security check would have been if he had paid into the system throughout his life. What happened to this man is that he kept hanging onto his church job. It was time for him to retire, and he could not retire because his annuity check would not cover his basic life necessities. If he had paid into Social Security and collected a monthly Social Security check, his monthly income together with his annuity would have been enough to have lived on. Sadly, he became sick and died while serving in his ministry. He never lived to deal with retirement, but he left a spouse behind who did have to deal with retirement. She did not have a vocation and would have collected whatever Social Security check he would have collected. The results are even more tragic because not only had he not thought about himself in retirement, he wasn't thinking about anyone else. I know in his heart that is not what he intended or wanted but, that became the reality.

Some churches are messing ministers up because they don't want to do what is right. Some churches don't want to pay their share of the employer Social Security tax. Some want to hand the minister $3,000 to $4,000 a year to pay their Social Security taxes quarterly, but this ends up being more money the minister has to report and pay tax on. Churches should W-2 all staff, including the pastor. They should do withholdings, pay the employer's share of the Social security tax, and the employees' share or whatever else is required. They can then give the minister a W-2 to file with his or her taxes. That makes it cleaner for everyone. Plus, in the long run, more money will eventually end up in the Social Security account of the minister.

Some churches are lazy when it comes to bookkeeping. They traditionally just want to hand a minister a check every week. They are happy to include, in the church budget, how much of the minister's salary is designated for car expense, house expense, library expense, medical expense, and all of that. Churches and clergy must quit the games. Every church should consider providing a medical insurance plan for their staff, even if the staff consists of one minister. There are insurance brokers who will help you figure it out. Or, you can buy into your denominational medical insurance plan if you are a part of a large denomination like Southern Baptists or Methodists.

A friend of mine, who served a congregation, that averaged over 2000, in Lexington, Kentucky, was close to retirement. He had served the church for over 30 years. He said to me one day, "Glenn, I hope my church gives me a retirement." I was not exactly sure what he meant but soon learned that he nor his church had paid into any kind of retirement plan or even an Individual Retirement Account. At that time, he was making about $70,000 a year, which was good but not great for a church the size he was pastoring. His church was a large, independent church and therefore did not have access to retirement plans provided by some denominations. For many years, Southern Baptists have had Guidestone, which has done a good job with the money invested by the ministers and churches of that denomination. At the end of this minister's long, long, tenure the church had a farewell service for him at Rupp Arena in Lexington, Kentucky. Rupp arena seats over 20,000 people. There was a large crowd who gathered that night to pay respect to him and listen to him talk. In that service, the church collected his retirement offering, which, I was told, was over $600,000. You can almost imagine this minister saying, "Whew,

God sent me that helicopter right before I drowned."

When he retired, in the nineties, $600,000 was a ton of cash. It is still more money than most people have saved toward their retirement today. If he and his church had systematically saved $1000 a month, and then more in his later years, he would have ended up with much more than $600,000. It would have felt like a much more respectful retirement than having to pass an offering plate to the entire community as your last official act of ministry.Unfortunately, some churches treat their ministers that way. My childhood pastor said, "Glenn, the church wants their minister to be humble and poor. God you keep them humble and we will keep them poor".

The minister and the church must understand that all lives reach a point where earning an income is not easy. It happens to all of us. We have to systematically put money aside every month for that time when we are no longer able to be employed. We all reach an age, if we live long enough, when we become too old, unhealthy, unwanted by others because of our age, or we just "don't" want to do it anymore. As I said previously, my dad retired from the mines at 55 after 30 plus years and never had any desire to do it again. That could happen to you in ministry, and that's okay. You may serve in ministry for 20 to 50 or more years and decide one day you don't want to do it anymore. You may not even want to fill in occasionally. You may reach a stage where you are happy to listen to someone else, play golf, fish, or even pursue another career for a while. There is nothing wrong with that. Everyone is wired differently.

God calls us all to serve him. He wants us to love him and to love people, but it does not mean you have to have a ministry job until you breathe your last breath. You can do something else and give someone else a chance to serve.

I know of ministers who say they are retiring at 65 or even 70 and go on to do 20 interim pastorates after they retire. They might as well have said, "I am not retiring." An interim pastorate has a different feel to the job because it is temporary and has fewer long-term expectations. The pay and benefits are not going to be as great either.

Often, ministers who are always doing interim pastorates, cannot function emotionally without knowing they have someplace to preach on Sunday. They have served a church for so long and gone through the daily rituals of visiting the sick and preparing sermons that the idea of totally not doing it is like a feeling of death to them. They can't figure out anything else to do with their lives or their new freedom in retirement.

Also, so many ministers do not save enough for retirement. They are hoping God will perform a miracle when they are old and take care of their needs. I have only heard of one minister receiving a miracle offering like my friend in Lexington. Most ministers get a Sunday lunch, with a few kind words from the church family, a silver platter, and maybe a little extra money for a vacation, if they are very lucky.

As I said, I started preaching when I was 16 years old. A little church in Denver, Kentucky, named Liberty Baptist Church, asked me to preach for them two Sundays a month. They had church two Sunday afternoons a month and about six to ten people in attendance. Driving from Milo road in Martin County, Kentucky, I became the visiting preacher. The drive was about 45 minutes over hills and winding curves to get to Liberty Baptist Church. They paid me $10 for gas every time I showed up. Harold Rice was the only deacon. He, his wife June, and their family were keeping the doors of the church open. I filled in two Sundays every month for over a year until the church decided to call me as their pastor. I agreed to serve, and they paid me $60 a month plus $6 a month for retirement. The denominational retirement board encouraged the churches or pastors to put 10% of their wages into the retirement fund. I certainly wasn't interested in retirement at the age of 17 and thought the $6 a month was a joke. That went on until I graduated from high school and moved on to Georgetown College and I took another church in Lexington, Kentucky. I probably served the church as the actual pastor for maybe a year. We had a good time. We baptized several people and grew to about 30 to 40 people on most Sundays. I got my papers from the Annuity Board of the Southern Baptist Convention that said that I was officially enrolled in their retirement program, and Mr. Rice faithfully made my $6 a month contribution to the Annuity plan.

For most of my life, I forgot about that $6 a month. The total contributions made by the church would have been less than $100 for the brief time I served in that capacity. One day I called the Annuity Board, now called Guidestone, and inquired to see what their record showed or even if a record still existed. I wasn't even sure if they would show if I had $6.00. Their records showed that I had over $27,000. I was floored. That little contribution had amassed an astounding amount of cash. Harold, his wife June, and the Liberty Baptist Church did something really great. They invested in a young preacher's retirement. They did a lot of great things like allowing me to preach and gain experience in ministry. What Harold Rice did in his tenacity to do the right thing is a shining example of what all churches should do for their ministers. Be tenacious about investing money toward the minister's retirement. Hopefully, it will be at least 10% of the minister's pay. Whatever you or the church set aside in retirement every month will be meaningful and helpful down the road. The quicker you do it, the longer that money has to grow. In my case, my little fund has had over 45 years to grow, which shows the power of compounded interest and not touching a retirement fund until your senior years. By the way, that $27,000 since I first checked on it has grown to $38,000. Who knows what will happen with the stock market. That fund may increase to $50,000 or more, all from a few monthly contributions of $6.00 a month. Let this sink into your head, my friend.

Another friend of mine sold a Universal Life insurance plan to me when I was about 26 years old. Interest rates were as high as 17% and greater back then. The idea with a Universal Life policy is that you are providing life insurance and also saving some money at the same time. I faithfully paid my premiums, and when I had a financially difficult period in my life, I had to cash it in. Over about 13 years that policy accumulated a cash value of over $7000 which was nice at a time when I needed it. However, I believe it is best to keep your life insurance and savings separate. Buy cheap term life insurance and save your money in a separate savings account, and you will end up having a lot more cash.

Back in the days of high interest rates, which would have been the early eighties, I heard a lot of presentations about how much money we could have in our denominational retirement if we saved at least 10% every month. At that time, if a minister was putting $5,000 a year into the denominational retirement plan, he or she was doing well. Actually, if you are doing that today, you are doing some nice saving because most people are not saving $400 to $500 a month. We received prospectuses that showed if we saved $400 to $500 a month, with interest rates being over 14%, that we would have well over one million dollars in our retirement accounts by age 65. That all looked good and sounded good, and many of us tried. One problem was that interest rates fell to almost nothing, and the stock market, which had such gigantic upward swings, had some significant falls along the way. Currently, the stock market has enjoyed a major surge. Millions of retirement accounts are experiencing nice inflated numbers, which will most likely decrease or have a fall, along with the stock market.

A friend of mine retired a couple of years ago. He paid into his denominational annuity plan most of his life. His amassed amount was about $350,000. He was very disappointed because his monthly retirement check was going to be so much less than what he had been living on. Another friend told me his fund had amounted to $450,000 at his retirement. Some saved much more, more consistently, and amassed greater amounts in their retirement funds. Some have made much more and could save more. Some made a lot and didn't save much at all. Some have made very modest salaries, but they sacrificed so they could save money and now have something to retire on. It is not about how much you make but about how much you can keep when it comes to saving money for retirement. All the people I know except for the one previously mentioned also collected Social Security money each month. The same rule applies to Social Security and retirement annuity accounts. You get out of them whatever you put into them.

One friend made a big salary for over 20 years and lived big. He had a big house and drove expensive cars, but he saved nothing for retirement. He ended up leaving his big house and moved into a family member's home. His Social Security check was almost nothing each month because he always reported a very low salary, which meant a modest income tax payment and a low Social Security tax payment. He had paid nothing into a 401(k) or even an Individual Retirement Account, so he had nothing to draw from. He spent his elderly years working minimum wage jobs, which included cleaning hotel rooms, working fast-food restaurants, retail, and any place that he could make a little bit of money to survive on. One day in his mid-eighties, he came home, sat down on his sofa, and had a massive heart attack. He loved his family and was a hard worker. He never took the importance of saving money for retirement seriously.

Consider all your options when it comes to retirement. Talk to your bank about an Individual Retirement Account. Talk to your denomination about any retirement plans they have. Most denominations now have retirement plans, and they pay people to spend time talking to people like you. They will help you, but you have to call them and make an appointment to meet with them. Numerous stockbrokers in shopping centers all over America and around the world will talk to you about investing in different stock plans. Talk to them and come up with some ideas for saving money. Put money in your bank. Usually, saving money in the bank is not the most fruitful in accumulating a lot of cash. Yet, many banks now have investment counselors who can guide you on Roth IRAs and other more productive retirements.

The main thing is to just do it. Do not talk about saving money. You must systematically do it every month. Even if you save a few dollars it's better than nothing. Sacrifice some to have something later. Drive an older car. Live in a modest home and do whatever is necessary to provide for your future. Make saving money every month a priority.

Even if you collect a respectable amount from your retirement savings and Social Security or whatever your government provides, you may still want to work some in retirement. Many do not, and do not have to. However, I see a lot of seniors running out of money in their senior years. Again, this is why so many ministers do interim work for churches. Many ministers stay with their work now up into their seventies and longer. I know of several pastors in their eighties and a couple in their nineties. They are still working and collecting full-time salaries. Most of them still enjoy writing sermons, making hospital visits, talking to people, and leading people to Christ. If you still enjoy your ministry and can physically and emotionally do the work and your congregation, or place you serve, will keep you, then why retire? You do not have to retire at 65 unless you are burned out and cannot do it anymore. Some congregations are more than ready for their minister to retire and are counting the days. That becomes a pressure that is unhealthy for your longevity. You need to get away from a toxic ministry and look for another place of service that is healthy for you and the congregation. Do not make this an excuse for not saving money. Keep saving money, even if you can serve or work until your eighties. Some ministers think they will keep working and not worry about saving money, but then they have to keep working because they did not save money. It will be a lot more fun to want to work because you enjoy the work than to work because you have to work to pay the utility bills. If you will save money every month, your workload will feel lighter instead of heavier as you age.

A lot can happen in life that may hinder consistent saving into a retirement plan. Sickness can eat away at any extra money you might have. Doctor bills can be massive and bankrupt thousands of families every year in the United States.

Some ministers connect into the right ministry and stay with it for 30 or more years and pay into a retirement plan the entire time and retire with a very comfortable monthly annuity. Many pastors and church ministry persons go through multiple ministries. If you serve 10 to 20 different churches and ministries in your lifetime but pay into the same retirement plan, it will still continue to grow throughout your life.

Ministers go through life crises just like everyone else. Life crises can range from personal problems, family issues, divorce, caring for aging parents, hurting children, mental/emotional breakdowns, and burnout. That is just to name a few. Life is seldom smooth throughout the entire journey. We face hurdles and challenges that can interrupt our ability to be productive or even work a job or serve in a ministry. That can significantly impact our retirement accounts. Remember, your retirement fund depends on faithful contributions. Making a few hundred dollars contribution now and then will not get the job done for you. If you have gone through a stressful period of your life that has interrupted your retirement, then refocus back on setting money aside once you get straightened out.

When I went to Gateway Baptist Church in Newburgh, Indiana, the church was very small and financially weak. There was not enough money to pay into a retirement account, and for the first two years, I paid nothing into retirement. As I said, my wife, Karen, was battling multiple sclerosis, and it was months before she was approved for Social Security disability. Medical expenses were incredible, and saving money was impossible. Fortunately for everyone, our ministry at Gateway grew, and in my last eight years with them, I was finally able to get back on track to invest a few hundred dollars each month into our denominational Guidestone account. That account will never be enough to retire on, but with Social Security and my writing, speaking, my Christian education work, preaching some, and so forth and the grace of God, I have hopes of keeping food on the table.

Lots of things can happen to impact our savings for retirement. One major negative is withdrawing money from your 401k or Individual Retirement Account or your denominational annuity. You can legally do so. The problem is you normally have to pay a 10% penalty plus the tax on the amount you withdraw. That ends up being a major financial negative. The biggest negative is what it does to the current and future balance of your retirement account. At midlife, I had to make a large withdrawal from my ministry retirement account to pay bills, and it sorely impacted my denominational retirement account. I recuperated quite a bit as I tried hard to catch up, but in reality, it's difficult, if not impossible, to completely catch up if you take a significant amount out of your account.

A dear minister friend told me about going through a divorce when he was 40 years old. He ended up cashing in all of his money that he had paid into his ministry denominational retirement account, to financially survive. Later in life, he had no real retirement account, but he never got back into the habit of saving money. He was able to make a living in his later years, but once he had depleted his retirement annuity, he never went back to saving money, which is a colossal tragedy.

An emotional issue that many parents are dealing with today is adult children. While in their mid-sixties, a minister friend of mine and his wife struggled financially, because they had a 40-year old son who required constant assistance. Actually, this pastor withdrew a lot of his annuity savings to help his son. The pastor never really recuperated financially from all the money that he and his wife had to continue to give to help their adult son.

Another pastor friend and his wife had an adult child, along with their grandchild, living in their home until she was in her forties. They took care of her and her child until they were financially broke and had to move out of their house and into a smaller place. The daughter finally found another place to live and means to support herself and her young child. The pastor and his wife never really recuperated financially.

Frequently, I see senior adult parents constantly handing out money to adult children for car expenses, apartment rent, house repairs, vacation money, food money, and the list goes on. Many of these senior parents get to the place where they spend their IRA retirement accounts and most of their extra saved money. They end up scraping financially, and of course, there is no one to help them.

For some reason, too many adults have led their adult children to believe they don't have to worry about anything and can always depend on them to be the ATM in their lives. That is a very bad scenario for parents and adult children alike.

One of the best things you can do to help yourself in retirement is to raise your children to be financially independent. I know many parents want to help their kids, and all of us should, to some extent. Many senior adults remember having it hard as young adults and try to save their children from the same pain. Yet, some of that pain is what makes you grow to be financially independent. You will struggle in retirement if your adult children are counting on you to see them through their financial hard times or simply to help them make their budgets each month.

Another friend was flat broke at the age of 50. He and his wife opened a hamburger stand, and they worked it 10 hours a day for over 15 years. The business became so successful that he and his wife ended up with about $300,000 a year income, and he retired very well and lived into his nineties. He and his wife served their church. They gave at least 10% to their church and also gave to other ministries. Their story had a good ending. The difference is that this man was not a pastor. He was a very active layman in his church and opened his own hamburger stand and did well. This story does not relate well to most ministers because ministries often limit or prohibit their pastors or staff personnel from doing much else that does not involve ministry. However, more and more ministers today are becoming bi-vocational, as many churches shrink in their financial ability to pay a full-time person. If you are bi-vocational and your place of ministry understands, you then have the flexibility to be creative and do work that might earn you a living income. This man's story gives hope to all who are a little late in life trying to still make a living.

Another friend outlived his retirement income. He collected $90,000 a year in retirement income. He told me that at the age of 90, his income would drop from $90,000 a year to his $24,000 a year Social Security. He lived to be 92 or two years past what he thought he would need to retire. To his credit, he lived an amazing life of generosity. During his retirement years, he often gave as much as half of his $90,000 away every year to his church and various ministries and charities. I know because he often wanted to show me a list of the places he gave money to and how much he gave. It made him feel really good that he was able to give that much money away, and so I listened to him talk about his giving. I don't think that is necessarily a great idea. However, here I am writing about him and his testimony of giving. So, it must not have been too bad for him to feel good about his giving. A point here is that he had worked hard his entire life. He had saved and invested his money. He lived in a relatively modest home for what he could have afforded, and he and his wife seemed happy.

Most ministers do not end up with big generous retirement funds. However, you can have a strong retirement fund if you plan, save money, and don't live for just today.

Take time today or this week and look over what your retirement is going to be. If you are in America, you can create a Social Security account online that will tell you very close to the penny what your monthly income is going to be. The account will show you what you have paid into it and what you will collect if you start collecting at age 62 or age 67. Talk to representatives for whatever else you are paying into and ask for a prospectus of what your monthly anticipated payout will be. Whatever denominational retirement plan, bank, stockbroker, or 401k you are investing in, take a periodic look at it to see if your account is growing and if it will be enough for you to live on when you want to retire.

Finally, you may be reading this book and be 27 years old or younger. You also may be 80 or even 90 years old. We do what we can and as we can when we can with what we have and can do. Our lives are different. Within each period of our lives, it is always prudent that we are good managers of what God has given to us. Whatever you save, has been given to you by the grace of God. Praise him and thank him every day. Thank him for every opportunity to work, have money, and to be able to save some money. Give to his work and others but be wise. You cannot give it all away and have anything. The 10% model of saving at least 10% and giving 10% away, is still a good model. If your income is extremely meager and you have very little to live on, keep in mind that you are living under the grace of God. God is not going to be mad at you if you use what little bit of money you have to feed your family instead of giving it to the church. Do the best you can. As God provides and blesses you, then give and do more whenever the time allows.

Chapter 9

Your Health

"But I will restore your health and restore your years says the Lord," Jeremiah 30:17

"Do you not know that your bodies are temples of the Holy Spirit who is in you, whom you have received from God? You are not your own: You were bought with a price. Therefore, honor God with your bodies." 1 Corinthians 6:19

"So whether you eat or drink or whatever you do, do it all for the glory of God." 1 Corinthians 10:31

"Do not be wise in your own eyes; fear the LORD and shun evil. This will bring health to your body and nourishment to your bones." Proverbs 3: 7-8

"He said, "If you listen carefully to the LORD your God and do what is right in his eyes, if you pay attention to his commands and keep all his decrees, I will not bring on you any of the diseases I brought on the Egyptians, for I am the LORD, who heals you." Exodus 15:26

"Worship the LORD your God, and his blessing will be on your food and water. I will take away sickness from among you," Exodus 23:25

"So do not fear, for I am with you; do not be dismayed, for I am your God. I will strengthen you and help you; I will uphold you with my righteous right hand." Isaiah 41:10

"Surely he took up our pain and bore our suffering, yet we considered him punished by God, stricken by him, and afflicted. But he was pierced for our transgressions, he was crushed for our iniquities; the punishment that brought us peace was on him, and by his wounds we are healed." Isaiah 53:4-5

"You restored me to health and let me live. Surely it was for my benefit that I suffered such anguish. In your love you kept me from the pit of destruction; you have put all my sins behind your back." Isaiah 38: 16-17

"And my God will meet all your needs according to the riches of his glory in Christ Jesus." Philippians 4:19

On hearing this, Jesus said to them, "It is not the healthy who need a doctor, but the sick. I have not come to call the righteous, but sinners." Mark 2:17

"Jesus went through all the towns and villages, teaching in their synagogues, proclaiming the good news of the kingdom and healing every disease and sickness." Matthew 9:35

"The righteous cry out, and the LORD hears them; he delivers them from all their troubles. The LORD is close to the brokenhearted and saves those who are crushed in spirit.

The righteous person may have many troubles, but the LORD delivers him from them all; he protects all his bones, not one of them will be broken. Evil will slay the wicked; the foes of the righteous will be condemned. The LORD will rescue his servants; no one who takes refuge in him will be condemned." Psalms 34:17-22

"My son pay attention to what I say; turn your ear to my words. Do not let them out of your sight, keep them within your heart; for they are life to those who find them and health to one's whole body." Proverbs 4: 20-22

"A cheerful heart is good medicine, but a crushed spirit dries up the bones." Proverbs 17:22

"There is a time for everything, and a season for every activity under the heavens: a time to be born and a time to die, a time to plant and a time to uproot, a time to kill and a time to heal, a time to tear down and a time to build, a time to weep and a time to laugh, a time to mourn and a time to dance, a time to scatter stones and a time to gather them, a time to embrace and a time to refrain from embracing, a time to search and a time to give up, a time to keep and a time to throw away, a time to tear and a time to mend, a time to be silent and a time to speak, a time to love and a time to hate, a time for war and a time for peace." Ecclesiastes 3:1-8

"LORD, be gracious to us; we long for you. Be our strength every morning, our salvation in time of distress." Isaiah 33:2

"Therefore, confess your sins to each other and pray for each other so that you may be healed. The prayer of a righteous person is powerful and effective." James 5:6

You can do anything if you take care of your health.

You can sell pencils if you have your health. When you are healthy you can pastor a big church or a small church, be a missionary and go to the remote parts of the world to share the good news of Christ. You can work a factory job, be in sales, farm, run your business, and then, do your ministry work in the evenings, and on weekends. When you lose your health, you don't feel good. You don't have energy. Your mental attitude changes as you are aware of a body that is not performing like it used to. Your focus is distracted from doing all the good things you would like to do like writing sermons, leading people to Christ, doing the work you want to do, and feel called to do because you don't feel good. Bad health leads to lots of problems. You can't give 100% to your job. You become preoccupied with the next doctor's appointment. You become distracted by mounting medical bills. If you are sick long enough and visit enough doctors and have procedures or surgeries, you most likely will have some hefty medical bills. A minister's salary often doesn't lend itself to large medical bills but neither does the average person's salary in the world.

More Americans go bankrupt over medical bills than any other reason. You can end up thousands and thousands of dollars in debt depending on the nature of your sickness or surgery. One lady recently told me that she needed surgery. She has medical insurance, but she would still end up with 30,000 in debt because of her deductibles and out of pocket expenses. A $30,000 debt was more than she could take on as a waitress.

After an extended hospital stay, a family member required monthly rehabilitation that insurance did not cover. At the time, the total cost was over $15,000 a month. Fortunately, her family had the money and paid $60,000 for four months of rehabilitation in a long-term care center. Most people today cannot come up with $60,000 out of pocket. Some would have to try to borrow the money from the bank or second mortgage their property if they had property. In most cases like this, the average person has to go on Medicaid. This means you don't have any money and it is government insurance that limits what they will pay for the patients. More and more stories are being told about rural hospitals and nursing homes closing up across America because so many of them have a majority of Medicaid patients. The Medicaid insurance does not pay what the hospitals and nursing homes charge and so they have to take less which means they have less to operate their hospital or nursing home on. The result has not been good for rural America as so many places that offered healthcare are now gone.

There are endless stories of people who needed surgeries and long-term medical care and could not get it because they did not have insurance or the money for their medical care. When you walk in the door of any doctor's office or hospital, in America, the first thing they want to see is your insurance card. Millions of senior Americans carry Medicare cards which have what is called a part A and a part B. Part A is automatically covered if you paid into Medicare throughout your life. Part B is something that is added and costs an additional premium every month. Part A pays for your hospital stay. Part B covers your doctor's visits and tests that you may have along the way with doctor's visits. On top of this seniors typically buy a prescription plan. This adds an additional cost every month. This is called plan D and not everyone carries this plan but any American who requires medicine is smart to take out the plan D prescription insurance at the time they receive Medicare. When it comes to medical insurance nothing will stay the same forever. The type of plans offered in America will continue to change over time.

When you are really sick, and you want to get well you can't start tabulating the cost. If you tabulate the cost, you are already behind the eight ball. You hope that the medical carrier will eventually give you a break and forgive some of the debt. You hope you can make small payments for the rest of your life or you hope some non-profit or foundation will help you. Your main concern is getting whatever treatment is necessary to help your family member or you. If you can live you can try to pay it back if they will give you the treatment. You can't pay anything back if you are dead.

Be realistic about your health. If you live long enough you will face something. Hopefully, it's not as major as multiple sclerosis or anything that requires a lifelong battle or a lifetime of care. However, any health issue is an issue that must be wisely monitored and medically treated. Ignoring a health problem is a recipe for disaster.

One of my dearest best friends was diagnosed with prostate cancer. He had medical insurance. He had money and he was a very smart man who was loved by almost everyone. He went to a local urologist who made the diagnosis but said for the meantime the cancer had not spread and that they would "watch it." This is a very common treatment among even the best of urologists and medical facilities throughout the country. It's called active surveillance. This concept is about having blood work done every few months and doing scans such as magnetic resonance imaging, commonly called an MRI. The patient is routinely monitored. If the numbers change, then at that time a more aggressive form of treatment is performed such as surgery or radiation. With my friend, they kept watching and watching and watching until they watched him die. From my perspective, he should have traveled to a different town and consulted with a different urologist, and moved forward on an aggressive treatment that could have extended his life for many years. In his situation, he was so busy with his ministry that he didn't take the time to medically care for himself. If he had taken three to six months for some aggressive treatment, his ministry may have continued for many more years.

His doctor did try some different treatments on him, but the treatments ended up being too late. The malignancy was already out of the prostate and eventually ended up in his bones.

Do not put off medical treatment. If you are diagnosed with cancer, a heart problem, diabetes, or anything serious, seek good treatment. Your local doctor may not be the best. He or she may be a nice person. They may give you a prescription every time you go, and they may be very caring, but they may be very limited in treating you. A good doctor will refer you to someone with more expertise than he or she has.

It's better to drive to a doctor 200 miles away and get good medical treatment than to stay with a doctor close to home and die. We look at travel as being inconvenient and expensive. The expense is what stops a lot of people. If you cannot come up with the gasoline money, then you can't go. However, if you can find a way to get to someone who is a better doctor, you are wise to try to find a way.

Take the time to do your research about what you need and what you don't need. The worst thing you can do is ignore this area of your life.

Food is a blessing and you should enjoy and give thanks for every meal God provides. Some people have problems with eating too much and often this is the Christian's favorite sin. Eating too much is something we feel we can get by with but it shows on us more than any other sin we commit. Some people become closet eaters. They will act like they aren't eating much, but then at night, after everyone has gone to bed, they eat like crazy.

Christians are to be good witnesses for Christ. I understand about being a stumbling block. I also know the opioid epidemic is killing massive numbers of people. This doesn't mean that I will never take a pain pill or seek other relief from pain if it is necessary. I understand that obesity and diabetes kill thousands of people every year, but this does not mean I will never eat pizza or ice cream again. People are killed on the highway every day in automobile accidents, but I hope to be able to drive for as long as possible.

Try to live a life of moderation in everything you do. Balance and organize your life so that you are in control and not something else. This is very important.

Many churches have thrown their hymnbooks away. I still love my old hymnbooks., but I like some good praise music too. Some folks think the King James Version is the only Bible and it may be for them. I have most of the versions and sometimes when I just want to relax and read an entire book in the Bible I'll pull out a Good News for Modern Man or The Living Bible. I have peers and mentors who act like they despise them both. Some people can't stand the King James Version of the Bible. I say we need to love the Savior of the Bible and that there is more in any of these versions that we can ever really fully grasp. We all have a lifetime behind us and maybe ahead of us trying to put into practice what we have already learned from or will learn reading God's word.

Inflammation is something that needs to be addressed when we start thinking about improving our health. Research shows that in combating cancer, arthritis, and most other diseases, inflammation in our bodies is the root of many of our problems. The foods we eat, especially the heavy sugar we put into our bodies, contribute to inflammation which may become the foundation for a lot of our problems. Cutting back or eliminating as much sugar as possible is one of the keys to dealing with the inflammation in our bodies.

Throughout my lifetime, I have eaten a lot of sugar. My Grandpa and Grandma operated Hinkle's grocery store which was directly across the creek and down the road from our family's home. It was about a 200-yard walk. I grew up drinking Pepsis, Cokes, RCs, all the Nehi drinks, and anything else my Grandpa was selling. He had shelves full of Reese's Peanut Butter Cups, Hershey's Bars, PayDays, Snickers, Zeros, and Zagnuts. He also had Honey Buns, Hostess CupCakes, pies, and a freezer full of ice cream. You are getting the idea. I grew up having access to all of this junk. My mom and dad kept a charge account that they paid every week. Often, my part of the bill was as much as $2 of junk that I bought throughout the week saying, "Charge it, Grandpa." Back in that day, soda pop was eight cents for a bottle. A candy bar or a small cake like a French pastry or honey bun was five cents. Ice cream was five cents and then ten cents for a long time. All of that changed and became much more expensive over time. However, all this ended after my Grandpa died when I was 15 years old. My Grandma closed the store soon after his death. Grandma died about a year later.

Pies and cakes were always in our home growing up. I don't remember them not being in the home of my parents except after my mother died. My dad did not eat as many sweets as my mother and the rest of my family. He ate some but he didn't feel like he had to have dessert in the refrigerator all the time.

My two sisters and my two brothers and I have eaten a lot of sugar over our lifetimes. I would hate to imagine how many pounds of sugar have gone through our bodies. It is a miracle we aren't all diabetic. None of the five of us at this point are diabetic which seems to be a miracle. However, in recent months I'm noticing my numbers are higher when my blood is checked. Now I'm watching my carbohydrates more closely. Over the years, we have curtailed our dessert eating. We still have it at family gatherings like Thanksgiving, Christmas, and family reunions. So, we are still eating some sugar.

Over the last year, I have made great strides personally in refraining from eating dessert. I have eliminated donuts and cookies from my diet along with the french fries and potato chips. This is a major life change for me. My doctor and all that I have researched have nothing good to say about the intake of food containing sugar.

One report said that when you eat sugar it's like pouring gasoline on cancer. Sugar is adding inflammation to your body that you don't need and energy to cancer cells that you do not want.

I have been told about and I have read many articles about the benefits of eating fruit. Fruit has plenty of sugar but eaten in moderation is good for us. It has natural sugar which is healthy for us as opposed to the refined sugar that most desserts and junk food items contain. So far, the only fruits my doctor told me to not eat are grapes and pineapple which he said are too sweet. Before he told me this, I was eating a small bowl of fruit every day crammed full of grapes and pineapple. They are so sweet and so good. I have limited myself to power fruits like blueberries, strawberries, oranges, blackberries, and occasionally watermelon, and other fruits.

Almost every day for the last year I ate the following: A handful of walnuts, a handful of blueberries, a cup of almond milk (30 calories in a cup), and at least two slices of whole-wheat toast. Make sure the label says whole wheat. Read on the label. You should avoid wheat-colored or just wheat or honey wheat. White bread in your diet will raise the insulin levels in your blood having the same impact as eating sugar. This is why you have to take a nap after eating a pizza. It tastes so good going down but after all that delicious thick crust is absorbed into your body it's going to give you a high and then a crushing low that makes you lethargic for a couple of hours and will probably lead to a big nap.

You will have to research and find out with your doctor what you need. Many doctors will never talk to you about vitamins, healthy eating, and lifestyle changes. Too many want to hand you prescriptions that the pharmaceutical representative is paying them to push off on you. Be very cautious about what your doctor is prescribing for you. Read about it, research it, and try to determine a way and time frame to get off whatever you are ingesting into your system. Sometimes you cannot as you may be stuck on a medication with no alternative, like thyroid medication or insulin.

I used to be an exercise junkie. I ran miles and miles, lifted weights, did aerobics, played basketball, and swam. I slacked off for a few years. I still tried to watch my food intake and even lost a bunch of weight eating yogurt the first part of every day, but I wasn't exercising. Carole and I would take a one-mile walk around the block every day, and I would do 40 to 60 push-ups in the morning or evening, 18 to 20 leg lunges, and a couple of squats. That was it for my routine. My routine was not terrible because most people aren't doing 40 to 60 push-ups, or lunges, or walking a mile every day. Too many people are merely thinking about a walk around the grocery store.

My exercise routine was not enough. When it comes to cancer and keeping your body healthy, the buildup of inflammation is one of our greatest enemies. We get inflammation through all kinds of sources. Inflammation is caused by stress, what we eat, and how we live. That's why healthy foods are so essential to fighting inflammation. Exercise is vital. Most experts say 20 minutes a day is all you need. If you are running a mile or two, it might be. In most cases, people are just walking the dog around the block for 20 minutes. While that is good, most people need a little more. Since exercise is such an important essential for your body's health, why not set aside 40 minutes to an hour for this important daily essential? You would give yourself an hour to watch a television show. Sometimes, you allow yourself an hour to eat. A part of your exercise for the day should include 15 minutes or so to recuperate. Drink plenty of water and eat some lean protein or fruit. That is vital in recuperating from the workout. I'm not saying you have to go full steam for 40 minutes to an hour. However, you need to pace yourself. Get your heart rate up, use your muscles, lift some light weights, and, when possible, walk fast or jog. Find ways to exercise more. Usually, we are so busy we cheat ourselves out of the time we need to exercise because we rush through it so we can move on to something else.

At the age of 63 and 64 I was diagnosed with thyroid and then prostate cancer. It would not surprise me if they both resulted from a couple of years of lax exercise. When I used to work out hard, I was sweating a lot, and a good sweat cleanses the body of a lot of physical and emotional toxins. During the couple of years that I wasn't exercising, I was making more trips to the donut shop, which is a poor substitute for exercise. Who knows for sure, but I have to be committed to exercise and healthy eating. You never know how much it will help for sure. One thing is certain, if we are lax in our eating and exercise, we will face the consequences.

God and our health are our greatest assets. If you have the power of God in your life and your health, you can climb mountains, swim rivers, build churches, grow mission organizations, lead multitudes to Christ and take care of your loved ones. You can sell sticks or rocks to make a living if you have to. You can do anything with God's help and your health. When you lose your health, you are greatly hindered in running the race that God has called you to run. You can run the race from a wheelchair, a walker, using a cane, or even from a bed, but your race will be very different. Once we are stationed in a nursing home bed or relegated to a corner of the house, where we seldom see other people because of our health, then our ministry will no longer be as dynamic or active. Of course, you can always pray and maybe read your Bible if you don't lose your sight. You can communicate the gospel if you don't lose your hearing or have a stroke, which leaves you unable to talk. Health is an amazing blessing. Even though you may do everything in your power to remain healthy, things can happen that take away your health.

You can also try like crazy to be healthy and still get run over by a car or hurt by a terrorist. You can have an emotional breakdown from all the stress that sometimes comes from ministry and trying to work with people who have a mental illness. That is another chapter.

These bodies are resilient, and they will last a long time if we care for them, but they will not last forever. Heart issues, cancers, and inherited health issues, passed down from one generation to another, are concerns for all of us. Something will take us down in our health, and at some point, something will take us all out of this world.

That doesn't mean that we should throw caution to the wind, eat and drink like crazy and live like idiots because we are going to die anyway. No, give life your best effort. You might live to be 80, 90, or who knows, maybe 100. Even if you do live to be 100 years old, you don't want to be curled up in some nursing home totally unaware of where you are or who you are.

Get sleep. Good sleep is always a part of good health. Eight hours of sleep is usually perfect. Seven hours of sleep is good, but under seven and you aren't going to function as well during your day. A lot of people try working and functioning on five hours of sleep. You aren't going to feel well, function well, or have much fun on five hours of sleep. If you get up at five in the morning, you need to turn off the television, cell phone, computers, and everything else and go to bed at nine. If you are only sleeping six or fewer hours at night, you probably will need a nap in the middle of the day. I went on a writing tear from the time I was 45 through about 48 years old and wrote seven books. I would wake up at two in the morning and sometimes write until five or six. Then I would help everybody else as I still had kids going off to high school or college and was taking care of Karen.

My pastoral ministry job at Gateway Baptist Church expected me to report in to my office normally no later than nine. It was a long day of doing all the things that pastors want to do and all the things people want us to do. Plus, I made trips back and forth to the house to check on Karen, feed her lunch, help her to the bathroom, do laundry, and be available to help with the kids. I can go on here, but the point is I was busy. Our church was growing. We had built a beautiful facility. We had big crowds of people. By two o'clock, in the afternoon, I was passing out from exhaustion in my office chair. Not often enough, unfortunately, but occasionally I would get a 10-minute nap that always helped me through the rest of my day that included meetings, caregiving, and anything that my children had going on. Often, many ministers try to run the race without any sleep. Your body will eventually shut down. Sometimes ministers get depressed and sleep too much. You don't need to be sleeping nine or ten hours a day unless you've been seriously ill.

Ministers aren't robots or superhuman. Exercise, eat healthy, pace yourself, and sleep.

Try to find ways to laugh. Laughter is healthy for anyone. Too often the ministry can be nothing but dead serious all the time. There are funerals, sickness, church stress, serious meetings, tension, and personality issues. All of this invades the minister's life and home. You cannot live with a dark cloud over your head. That invades your family and your home. Your family's home needs to be a happy place. Try to see the humor in life. See the humor in other people. Watch television shows that make you laugh. Learn to laugh with your friends and family. Find ways to laugh with each other as a family without laughing at each other. Keep each other in high respect but find the humor in your daily life. Laughing lifts the load. Laughing makes a dreary day a little brighter. A family that can pray together but also laughs together will be happier. That goes for your church as well, and you personally. It's healthy to see the humor and enjoy the chuckles along the way. That means that you will have to loosen up a little and be willing to laugh at yourself.

I've had a few friends who made me laugh every time we talked. They are the ones I always looked forward to talking to the most.

One lady has been one of our best friends for many years. She laughs a lot. As I write these words, she is 99 years old. She works in her garden from spring to fall. She tills the ground by hand and works every day that she can. Up until a year ago, she mowed her small yard with a push lawnmower. She eats a lot of vegetables that she grows and not a lot of meat. She lives on a meager retirement income in a small house where she has lived most of her life. She drove her car until she turned 99. She still shops at her local grocery, goes to have her hair fixed, and is a greeter at her church. She is a beautiful witness for Jesus. She is an amazing woman with a wonderful personality. More and more, I would like to be like her. However, her genes are good. She takes almost no medicine except an occasional blood pressure pill. She's never had cancer or anything else wrong with her that I know about. Health is on her side. That is something that few of us can say, because by the time we hit 50 years old, issues can start slipping up on us.

My dad was diagnosed with colon cancer when he was 60 years old. It could have killed him, but he survived having a major part of his colon cut out and lived 25 more years. Sometimes, even by the time you are in your early forties, colon polyps are growing in your colon that can become malignant. Diabetes can start working on your body at an early age and can kill you at an early age if you don't treat it and take care of yourself. People develop fatty livers at an early age because of bad eating and alcohol habits that take them out of life at an early age. So, our 99-year-old friend has been very blessed. However, she was still jogging when she was 70 years old and still exercises in her house every day. She doesn't jog anymore, but she is constantly touching her toes, moving her arms, and stretching on the floor. However, I have to think she is truly blessed with some good genes and a lot of the grace of God as well.

Do all you can do to eat healthy, exercise, and see your doctor for routine blood work and checkups. Do everything you can to have medical insurance so that you don't ever feel like you can't go to the doctor. Live healthy, think healthy, and be healthy within your mind, heart, and soul. Be healthy and at peace with other people. Be especially healthy in your daily walk with God.

Chapter 10

Your Salary

People have different attitudes about the minister's salary. Some believe that the servant of God is worthy of his or her hire, as long as the servant of God does not earn as much as they do. Some believe the minister should earn much less than they do. Occasionally you will find people who have the attitude that it is okay for the minister to make as much money as they earn. And then you will find a few who will realize that it's okay if the minister has a bigger salary than theirs.

People have to realize there are different income levels of life. A retired person living on Social Security and income from a 401 (k) or some other work-related income may have enough to live on comfortably. They may also be 65 or 70 or older and should have their house paid for or at least their living space secured and children raised. They can't expect a pastor, at the age of 35 or 45, to live on what a retired person is living on. Medical insurance is expensive, and families are expensive. Saving for retirement, paying for children's education, affording a car, and going to the grocery store all add up. A minister cannot save for retirement if his or her church will not or cannot pay the minister enough to save for retirement.

The minister will have quite a lifelong journey with committees, teams, elders, deacons, or whoever pays the salary.

Much of the time, it will be frustrating. Not always. But unless you have your own church and decide your own salary, you are at the mercy of the church finance committee or personnel committee or whoever decides how much money they are going to let you have to live on.

Some people believe the minister is never supposed to think about money. If the minister thinks about money, then he or she is carnal, worldly, and his or her heart is not right. Some have the attitude that somehow God supernaturally takes care of the minister. They think God directly pays his or her bills like the electric bill, gas bill, water bill, sewage bill, telephone bill, Internet bill, car payment, gasoline, groceries for the family, housing, and so forth. In this day and age, this is probably hard for most people to believe, but if you've been in ministry for some time, you know there are all kinds of mentalities out there regarding the minister's pay.

Hopefully, most of the people you come into contact with in ministry realize that you are a human just like they are and that the ox that treads out the grain deserves his or her reward.

As a teenager, I had some interesting discussions with my father. He was a coal miner and made a lower-middle-class living. We had more than many people because my dad worked so many hours in the coal mine. One of my aunts said, "Glenn, your dad makes more money than anybody in Martin county." It was weird that she thought that because I knew it wasn't true. In 1975, his last year as a coal miner, he earned in the upper

$14,000 range. We had so many people in Martin County who did not work jobs and many who lived in outright poverty. So whatever income that anyone made seemed large to others. That is often how it is in the church. You have people with all kinds of socioeconomic situations who may see your minister's pay as being lucrative. While it is most likely not, it appears that way to them.

I started preaching when I was 16 years old. Between the ages of 16 and 18, my mom and dad, and I had several conversations about where I was going. These conversations entailed two vastly different perspectives. They had attended churches their entire lives that never paid their pastors a dime. Their pastors were always strictly volunteers. Their church was so small that keeping the electric bill paid was an endeavor.

The church where I was baptized and attended provided a parsonage and a salary to our pastor. I was aware of other churches that took care of their pastors. Some did well and some struggled. I knew, at a young age, that the path I was on was not going to be anything lucrative. Even in the best of situations, a ministry job was not a get-rich job, and most of the time, ministers struggled to make ends meet. My parents saw this much better than I did. My father said, "Get a good job and preach on the side." He was all for me going to college and becoming a school teacher or doing whatever I could get a job doing. My parents were not against me preaching or pastoring a church, but they couldn't see that I would ever be able to take care of myself as a minister.

Looking back, mom and dad had some legitimate concerns. Most parents do. It's funny how, as young people, we think we know more than our parents. My parents were very concerned. Plus, I was looking at Georgetown College, which is a very expensive, private college in Kentucky. At that time, they were connected to the Kentucky Baptist Convention, but they are no longer.

My mom and dad were not steering me wrong. I could have become a bi-vocational pastor and done well. I would later see pastors who maintained full-time jobs and even pastored large churches and did well. That has been rare. When they get to a certain size, most churches demand that their ministers work full time for them. With so many small and medium-sized churches who know they cannot pay much salary, the bi-vocational part-time minister is in demand.

I felt like I could make it as a full-time minister and did for some time, but often it's a long haul to achieve. I was in small churches until I was 26 years old and medium-sized churches mostly after that. Three of my last churches grew significantly. We built buildings, reached a lot of people, gave a lot to missions, and did more than any of them had ever done before. I would estimate though out my 40 years of mostly pastoral ministry that I had about 20 years that I made a medium-level income in comparison to what medium incomes were during those periods. In a way, that was good. But in a way, it was not so good. Like me, most ministers start out in small churches. It usually takes a long time to grow your church to the point where they can pay you more. Often, it takes a while before you can move to a church that can pay you more. However, with time, you can. Many ministers have to make a move before they can get a raise in pay. It is sad to have to uproot your family and move across the state or to another state to get a pay raise. Sometimes the raise might not be that big.

When you are serving a church, and you are concerned about what your salary is going to be, you have to determine who in the church makes more money than you. You have to determine if these people are on your side and like you. You then have to do whatever it takes to have these people placed on the finance committee of the church or whatever committee determines your salary. You can't have the poorest people in the church on the finance committee. You certainly cannot have the people in the church who may not like you on your committee. A committee consisting of people who make more money than you will look at what is in the budget for the salary and realize you don't have much to live on. If enough money is coming into the church, they will increase your salary. Some congregations vote on budgets, and more churches allow their leadership committees and teams to decide on salaries and budgets. If you start your own church and have control of the church finances, to some extent, you can pay yourself whatever the inflow of contributions will allow.

When I was in small churches, most of my salary raises amounted to about $2000 a year, and I was thrilled. When you aren't making much, any increase is helpful. Some of the more full-time churches I served later would often increase my compensation by about $4000 a year. Normally, I had to spread this out between salary, car allowance, retirement, and other expenses. Any raise was never just a straight salary increase.

Every church I ever served grew every year. Even the small churches would add 40 to 50 members a year. One church I served had only had 20 additions in the prior five years. We had 40 additions in the first year I served. I'm saying this in all praise to God. I do not want to simply toot my own horn. God blessed us with church growth every place I served.

When the finance committee gathered to review and make recommendations about salary, no one could ever say I didn't deserve one. I worked hard. I visited. Every day I was on the lookout for someone I could lead to faith in Jesus Christ. I baptized regularly. I worked hard on sermon preparation. I always tried to be kind and friendly to people so that there wasn't much reason to say I didn't deserve an increase in compensation.

In my first couple of years at Gateway, the pay wasn't much at all, but we grew rapidly. I finally got people on the committee who all had good jobs and made more than I did. The fourth year I was there, they gave me about a $9,000 increase. That was a major bump, and it really helped me. Almost every year I was there, my increase was at least $4,000 or so, and I was there for ten years. By the time I was ready to move from there to pursue building and growing Newburgh Theological Seminary, Gateway Baptist had a very nice pastor's compensation package to pass on to the next pastor. Whether or not they gave it to the next pastor, I do not know. Many churches start seeing how big the pastor's financial package is and start trying to hire the next person at a much lower salary.

Different variables go into how much your minster's salary will be. The size of your congregation. The financial income of your congregation. The attitude of the leadership of your congregation. Are most of your people retired and living on Social Security or other fixed incomes? Are they mostly young people who are starting out and have not had a chance to increase their income yet? How well is your church doing in reaching people? Are you growing? Are you dying? Is your church a happy church? Is your church a healthy church? If your church is filled with dissension and in-fighting, this creates an environment that disables growth, stifles giving, and lessens the chances that you are going to get much of a salary increase. Internal bickering never creates an environment that rewards the ministers and staff personnel of the church. In this environment, if an increase is given, then it's usually given with some resentment or consternation. That is not healthy, for the long term, for the staff or the church.

There are expenses every minister and every church have to consider. Your base salary. Your housing support, whether it's a parsonage or housing allowance. Housing allowances must include utilities. Car expense. Ministers spend a lot of time in their cars. Your health insurance. Don't try living without health insurance. More bankruptcies are tied to medical bills today than any other cause. Retirement. Contribute every month faithfully to a denominational or Individual Retirement Account that can be set up in most banks. Eventually, you may want to move this over to Ameritrade or some similar company where you will have more options on stock funds that you select and control. Some banks have counselors that can guide you with an IRA fund that may produce more than a small trivial interest rate. Don't invest in a fund that is going nowhere. Eventually, you want your monthly income to get the highest rate of return possible.

Book allowance. Travel and meal allowance. Convention and conference allowance. Continuing education allowance. These are all areas of expense that the average minister confronts. When the finance committee and you are talking about these expenses, be prepared to relate what it costs you to operate a cell phone. Tell them how much medical insurance is costing your family. Be prepared to say, "I only contribute this small amount a month to my retirement. I'm going to retire in poverty." They can't expect you to retire in poverty.

When you have good people, who are in the know, on your committee or leadership team, you won't have to explain medical insurance, cell phone costs, and what it costs to travel or live on. They will know because they face it every day.

The best people I ever had on any of my fiancé committees were business people. They were people who owned or who were involved in businesses. They had a grasp of what it took to make a business work and succeed. They knew what it took to live on and what it took to operate and sustain a business. Often business people see the church as a business and know you have to take in money and spend money, and you have to have good people working for you to make the business successful.

Some of the worst people I ever had in leadership were medical doctors. Some of them had a God syndrome. They thought because they had become doctors that they were God and knew everything. Sadly, some of them didn't think the minister should make anything close to what they were making. That, of course, does not hold true for every medical doctor. Some of my dear friends have been doctors down throughout the years. I'm saying this so that you might be aware. Often young professionals just starting out are begrudging of what the minster makes. Possibly the minister is 50 years old, and it has taken him a long time to get to where he or she is in their salary earnings. A young professional just starting out has not reached their salary potential and won't for some time. They join the church and see how much the minister is making, and they are aghast. "Oh my goodness!" They exclaim. "The minister is making more than me!"

As a minister, you don't want this person on your committee for many years down the road. They need time to grow up and see that it's okay for other people to make a little more money than they do. However, often the church is so desperate for leadership that they snatch up young professionals and put them on every leadership committee of the church. It is a big mistake to hand over the leadership of the church to people who have just walked in the door. Give people time. Find out who they are. Observe their attitudes and commitment to the Lord and how they live their lives before you give them the kingdom. People need a year of membership before they receive a committee assignment in the church. It's good for everyone to serve, but often we think service is being on five committees in the church. Service needs to begin with helping people, community benevolence, and support roles in the church. That gives them time to get to know the church and for the church to know them.

In time you and other leadership members of the church will be able to identify the talents and gifts of whoever has joined the church, whatever their background is, and how they might better serve. Some may be suitable for leadership, and others may not. You may want some on your finance team and others you may not.

Chapter 11

Your Availability

"After He had sent them away, He went up on the mountain by Himself to pray. When evening came, He was there alone," Matthew 14:23

"Early in the morning, while it was still dark, Jesus got up and slipped out to a solitary place to pray. Mark 1:35

"In those days, Jesus went out to the mountain to pray, and He spent the night in prayer to God." Luke 6:12

"About eight days after Jesus had said these things, He took with Him Peter, John, and James, and went up on a mountain to pray." Luke 9:28

"And as He was praying, the appearance of His face changed, and His clothes became radiantly white." Luke 9:29

Technology is ever-changing. That is good and sometimes not so good for ministers. Advances in communication such as cell phones, text messaging, live video chats, and messages that come from email and social media can be very convenient but also challenging.

I haven't had an active staff church job for a few years. Back when I did, cell phones were exploding onto the scene but were limited to conversations and were very expensive. Most of the time, they were used only when necessary. Today, most everyone spends their lives staring at their phones. People walk down the streets holding their phones. People have dinner sitting around the table with their telephones in hand.

If you have a ministry-related job and 200 or 2,000 people know your cell phone number or have access to you via social media, you might go crazy. You can't have a life with this kind of accessibility.

Today, people can "friend" their minister via social media and send him or her messages about anything and everything that is going on. That can become tough on the pastor's schedule. I've had people in previous churches almost drive me crazy by calling me about anything and everything. One senior adult woman came by the church office three or four times a week to spend 20 to 30 minutes talking about nothing. It got to the point where I had to try to plan my schedule to avoid her. It's hard for pastors to do sometimes.

One tremendous help is a secretary or staff member who will guard your time. They can say, "The pastor is studying now and won't be available for another hour." They can take messages. They can say, he is on the telephone or doing research or whatever you are doing. Your investment in a good staff assistant will be one of the best investments you can make in your ministry.

The minister who is always available 24/7 isn't going to be worth much. You can't always be on call, answering every message, responding to 20 different people texting you, or more in a day. You can only respond to so many emails and answer so many calls. If you don't have some boundaries in your communications life, you won't have much of a life at all, nor will your family.

A good staff assistant can answer some of your emails, take telephone calls, and relay messages. The wrong secretary or staff assistant can mess you up in a big way depending on whether she or he likes or dislikes you. Make sure that whoever is in this position is on your side and supportive of you. Often leadership within the church chooses who they want to be in the church office, including the secretary or secretaries. Today, these support staff personnel may be called secretaries, ministry assistants, or something else. Sometimes these people are strictly working for the church and doing their church jobs and don't feel necessarily committed to the minister having a life or being successful in his or her ministry. Often a church secretary develops loyalties to a few of the leaders in the church and ends up being a reporter to them of what you are doing every minute of the day. That is not necessarily a bad thing and can be a good thing. It all depends on the secretary's personality and the people who want to be in the know of every move you make.

A staff person can report on your whereabouts and spin it in a multitude of ways. "Yes, the pastor is gone right now. He is gone all the time, it seems." Or, "Yes, she is at the hospital, sure seems like she is at that hospital all the time." Or, "The minister is out visiting today seems like he visits a lot, but I don't know where he is or who he is visiting." Or, "Yes, she is in her study and doesn't want to be bothered. Oh, I don't know for sure what she is studying. She sure spends a lot of time studying." A good assistant will put an upbeat spin on whatever you are doing if they are any good at all. If they are working against you, then no matter what you are doing, even if you are on your knees in fervent prayer, they will find a way to respond in an unsupportive tone. And, if you have a negative or unsupportive assistant, you will probably be on your knees in prayer a lot more than usual.

People today don't want to talk to assistants or secretaries, but they will get used to it if you say this is how it is and stick with it. There will be many people in your ministry who think they are above going through someone else and will want direct access to you. Warn them upfront that there are hours in the day when you turn off your social media, cell phone, text messaging, and everything else. Let them know there are hours in the day for you and God. There are also times when you are visiting with a dying person in the hospital, and you don't need a cell phone call or some buzzing text or email coming through on your phone. Turn it off when you are in the funeral home, talking with people, at the hospital, praying, and preparing sermons. People can leave a message if it's important. Emails and texts will show up later when you turn your phone back on.

I'm not suggesting that you be rude, disrespectful, or arrogant. I'm talking about your life, ministry, and your sanity. You have a right to have a healthy ministry. Just because you are in ministry and working for a group of people does not give them the right to invade your life when and however they choose. Some of your people will balk at this, especially when "they" need you. The rules are okay as long as they don't apply to them. When they are applied to your lead Elder or chairman of your deacons, then you may get some static, but the rules really should apply to all.

You will have to let people know that you check email, text messages, and voicemails regularly. That will let them know that you will, in time, communicate with them. If you have social media, messaging, and all of the latest methods of communication, you will have to eventually respond or have someone respond for you. You can't get by with not responding to people in a ministry position. Keep in mind with all of these suggestions that you must always use common sense.

My doctors at Cleveland Clinic respond to me via email. It may be a day or two later, and the message may be brief, but everybody I've ever emailed has emailed me back. Sometimes it's been one sentence or five or six words, but they did respond. That always impresses me. Keep your communication to the point, and it won't be so overwhelming.

You will still spend a lot of time on the telephone, emailing, and probably text messaging. So many people want to communicate via text messaging today. The thing about text messaging is that someone can interrupt your sleep, your dinner time, your day off with a text message. I heard about a man who took a job and moved from Ohio to California because the company promised he would never receive a phone call, text message, or email after five o'clock. For several years, the company stayed committed and fulfilled their promise to him.

A minister is never going to get that promise from a church or ministry who hires him. The big thing with ministry is, "I might need you. Can I call you when I need you? We need a minister who is available all the time."

Down throughout the years, the church has gone too far, insisting on ministerial availability and accessibility. The church always has several needy people and several people with mental health issues. We live in an age where there are a lot of mental health problems. Mental health problems have been around a long while. Quite a few individuals with mental health issues sit in the pews of most of our churches.

Most every minister has a handful of people who call him or her every day needing to talk, needing advice, needing prayer, is depressed, or simply wants attention. Somehow you have to eventually let them know that you cannot talk with them every day. Advise them that many, many people are sick, in the hospital, need prayer, as well as prospects to contact. You can't talk to him or her every day. Hopefully, you can try a commonsense approach with this person and agree to 15 minutes to talk, once a week. Some of these people will agree to that and say it's a wonderful idea. But, they will still call you every other day because they suddenly found out something that you need to know or something that God has laid on their heart for you to know.

With these people, you will have to pray and seek God's wisdom and try to find a way to minister to them without saying something mean to them. You don't want to do that. People can irk you and test you emotionally. Don't let them push you to the brink of saying or doing something crazy. You will be the one who looks bad, and you will be criticized by your congregation. Find ways to shut off your telephone, any messaging media that interrupts you, and have hours that everyone understands is your time for study, planning, and organizing.

Make sure you have your day off committed and understood every week for you, your spouse, and your family. Guard this time and stick to it for the sake of your personal and marital health.

"Jesus often withdrew to lonely places and prayed," John 5:16. Jesus knew the importance of finding a quiet place to get away by himself to be free of distraction. Can you imagine if Jesus and the crowds who followed him all had cell phones and social media? Find a place where you can think, pray, work, and turn everything off. People do not have to know where you are all the time. It may be a place only your spouse or friend knows about, but it's a place where you can think, be quiet and hear what God is saying.

"After He had sent them away, He went up on the mountain by Himself to pray. When evening came, He was there alone." Matthew 14:23. Jesus didn't take his disciples with him. There are those times when ministers are so depleted they need a little time when no one is talking to them. I used to feel that way on Sunday nights. We would have 700 or 800 people on Sunday morning who I would shake hands with, and then maybe 150 would come back on Sunday nights, and I would preach and do it all over again. Normally, there was at least one meeting of some kind every Sunday. Sundays for me always started at six AM, looking over my sermon notes and practicing my sermon in my head. By the time church was over on Sunday night, I usually had spent about 14 hours going over two sermons, delivering two sermons, being there for Sunday school, meetings, and often something after church. Sunday is typically a long day for most ministers. That is just how the job works. Or, today, it may be a long weekend. Churches have Saturday night services, very early Sunday morning services, and late morning Sunday services. For a minister in a ministry such as this, the schedule is stretched thin.

"Yet the news about him spread all the more so that crowds of people came to hear him and to be healed of their sicknesses. But Jesus often withdrew to lonely places and prayed. One day Jesus was teaching, and Pharisees and teachers of the law were sitting there. They had come from every village of Galilee and Judea and Jerusalem. And the power of the Lord was with Jesus to heal the sick," Luke 5: 15-17 Note here the power of the Lord was with Jesus to heal the sick. He probably had been to that quiet place to pray and rest up, and he was ready now to offer something to the people. If you are always tired, drained, and available, you aren't going to have a very powerful presentation.

Pace yourself, rest, turn off your cell phone, social media, and email at certain times like dinner with your family and times during the evening. Have time off. Take care of yourself physically, mentally, and most of all spiritually. You aren't a superman or woman. You may be super, but you are human, vulnerable, and not invincible. The crowds can overtake you. Enough people can eventually get to you, wear you out and even end your ministry. Enough people got to Jesus, and they hung him on a cross. He overcame the grave, and we are better for all he did through the cross and his resurrection. Keep in mind that one cross was and is enough. You don't need to be on a cross and overtaken by the masses.

Do the best you can and be a good minister. You can do it with God's help, wisdom, and the power of his Holy Spirit, filling you and guiding you. Go for the long race. In a long race, you pace yourself. You don't try to win the race in the first few minutes, but you run wisely and don't burn yourself out in the first couple of miles. That applies to your work and your accessibility. Be accessible, but not all the time. Be present, but not all the time. When you are there, be all there. Rest, commune with God, love him and your family, and then give it your best wherever you are and whatever you are doing in serving him.

Chapter 12

Do Not Be the Hired Gun

"Humble yourselves before the Lord, and he will lift you up," James 4:10

"In the presence of God and of Christ Jesus, who will judge the living and the dead, and in view of his appearing and his kingdom, I give you this charge: [2]Preach the word; be prepared in season and out of season; correct, rebuke and encourage— with great patience and careful instruction. [3]For the time will come when people will not put up with sound doctrine. Instead, to suit their own desires, they will gather around them a great number of teachers to say what their itching ears want to hear. [4]They will turn their ears away from the truth and turn aside to myths. [5]But you, keep your head in all situations, endure hardship, do the work of an evangelist, discharge all the duties of your ministry," 2 Timothy 4: 1-5

"He has made us competent as ministers of a new covenant— not of the letter but of the Spirit; for the letter kills, but the Spirit gives life," 2 Corinthians 3:6

"and will give our attention to prayer and the ministry of the word." Acts 6:4

"to equip his people for works of service, so that the body of Christ may be built," Ephesians 4:12

Every minister should insist upon a job description. You need this before beginning to serve any church or ministry. That needs to be upfront, in writing and documented with the committee or the hiring person. The committee needs to sign your job description. If the church votes on your employment, a copy of your job description signed by the hiring committee should be presented to the church. This way, the church knows what you are supposed to do, and you know what you are supposed to do. That should be done for the pastor, associate pastor, and any minister or staff person of the church. If the job description is changed and the church voted on it when they hired you, they need to vote on it again. The committee signs it, and you sign it.

Most churches have not done this, and many never will. They will point to a few passages of scripture and say this is the kind of man or woman we want. They will list several general overall expectations that they have of you that will include preaching good sermons, visiting the sick, doing funerals, weddings, growing the church, winning people to Christ, conducting baptisms, communion, going to the hospital, supervising the staff, and whatever else the committee members happen to think of during the interview. Many churches have constitutions or bylaws that haven't been updated in years, but they hold to them as though they are sacred literature-sometimes. Often the church bylaws are dusted off when someone feels the need to circumvent something that is about to take place in the church.

A difficult ministry is when you have people in leadership who have input and impact on your life by changing the expectations routinely. Your ministry can be going in what you think is a stable, smooth pattern, and then you start hearing that you should be doing something else. Or, someone who is power-hungry and needs attention tells you that you need to do more of something and less of something else. In today's world of ministry, it could be almost anything.

Years ago, I was called to a church that had staff members who were loved by some and hated by others. Some of the church desperately wanted those staff members out, and some were committed to keeping them. The committee that hired me was vague about the staff. One lady said, "You have to meet the staff," but said it while rolling her eyes and shaking her head. Once I got to the church, I started having people visit me in my study to express disdain for the staff and wanted them out of the church. There were multiple reasons given. Some did not like them on a personal level. Some thought they had poor skills. Some thought they were ineffective. Some did not like their demeanor. Some thought they made too much money and were jealous of their salary package. Some had engaged in conflict with them, and heated rhetoric was exchanged. These people were constantly pressing me about something concerning "those staff people."

A pastor or any minister never wants to be in a position of refereeing people. It's a no-win situation. Everybody has some support, no matter how ineffective they are or how many people are against them. As a pastor, I didn't have the authority to terminate anyone and didn't feel I needed that authority. The deacons ended up having numerous meetings where people argued about these staff members. One guy even stood and pounded the table and yelled at the other deacons about the staff situation. Overall, the group was committed to terminating the staff members and drew up a letter offering them a severance if they would leave. The offer was accepted.

That was a very unhappy, pressured time which took place in the first year of a new ministry. That was a lousy way to begin a new ministry in any church for any minister. The leadership of the church should have taken care of this problem before I got to the church. If staff needed to be terminated, they should have done so without hanging this noose around a new minister's neck. The termination was something the church never really got over. We moved on and eventually hired new staff. We grew in leaps and bounds and added hundreds and hundreds of new members to the church.

However, there were six or seven people in that church who seethed during my entire ministry about the termination of those staff members. They were not a problem I created. They were a problem that the majority of the church wanted to have resolved. The deacons, who were the leadership of the church, took care of the termination. I still got much of the blame, and some of the church leadership said that it was my call and that the deacons were simply making the staff change to help me. In reality, I came to the church to preach the gospel and do the Lord's work. I didn't come to the church to be the church boss or the church bad guy.

A lot of churches want the minister to ride into town and be the hired gun. In the old days, if there were villains that needed to be taken care of, the town might employ a hired gun to come in and take care of business. He would come in and shoot this one down, then he would shoot another one down, and then he would shoot a few more down. The problem with this is that the hired gun almost always gets shot. The minister who allows the cowardly leadership of his church to force him to be the hired gun is making a big mistake. You will end up being the one that will be wounded, and it may be fatal.

Ministers have a job to do, and that is the ministry that God called you to do. Your work is the Lord's work. You obviously must be involved in whoever the church hires since you must work together as a team. Teams can win, and teams can lose. Winning teams and winning ministries work together in love, humility, and harmony. You may not always agree, but you have to agree to disagree and move forward supporting, and helping each other to carry out the work of the ministry.

If possible, begin your ministry with a written understanding of what is expected of you. When the leadership wants you to start leaning heavily on someone or some group in your church, then you and they fully understand this is the work of the Elders, the Deacons, a committee, but it's not your job. You will almost always be asked, "What do you think about this?" "What is your opinion?" "What should we do?" That is another way that people can drag you into a power struggle. They will then report, "Our minister or our Associate thinks this is what we should do." If your opinion is not what the leadership wants to do, then your opinion may not be reported. If you do not want to do the dirty work, they may accuse you of not being a leader. One of the nebulous methods that many churches and ministries use to chisel away at a pastor or ministry staff member is to accuse them of being a poor leader. Leadership is in the eyes of the beholder. A good leader, to some, may not be a good leader to others. Usually, in the minds of people, you are being a good leader if you are doing what they think you should be doing. What they think you should be doing may be good or it may not be so good.

You have to minister and work as God wants you to work. Your calling is from God. You are a servant of God. The church or organization writes your check, but you have to remain faithful in looking to God in prayer and for his direction. If you please God it doesn't matter who you displease. If you don't please God, it doesn't matter who you please. Sometimes you will do everything you can, to simply try to do what God wants you to do, and some people will not be happy. There will be times that you will make a few people happy but will fail God. God is your authority. He called you to ministry, and he is the one who opens doors for you to serve and minister to others. If your ministry does not work out in one place because you tried to do the right thing, God will provide another place of service.

Do not let a group in your church manipulate you into doing their dirty work or being the bad person. They will want to talk about your authority. They will want to say that you are the authority. After you have carried out whatever they wanted you to do, they can easily turn around and change the rules and remove your authority. Even if you are in a large church or even if you are a controlling board member of your ministry, shy away from the things that someone else should do so that you can take care of the work God has called you to do.

Of course, there are always those unique crises where you have no choice but to sink or swim. You have to take a stand and express the right thing to do about the issue. Then, you have to let the chips fall where they do.

We were voting on a new sanctuary at Gateway in Newburgh, Indiana. Many wanted it, and many did not. We were almost in gridlock. At that time, the church needed it, and I knew we could build the facility. The day we voted on whether to move forward or not, I preached my entire sermon in support of voting to build. To build we needed a 75% majority to vote in favor, which looked doubtful. When the votes were counted after the sermon, the vote to build passed by two votes beyond the 75% required. We built a beautiful new facility that became a marvelous place to worship. The only problem is that about 24% of the people never forgave me for taking that kind of stand for the new facility. If I had not taken a stand, Gateway would have retreated and maybe never built their worship facility. Several of those people who didn't get their way left for other churches. Some stayed with a commitment to be as unsupportive of me as possible for my remaining ten-year ministry at that church.

You have to decide what God is leading you to do. Try to do what you feel is the right decision for the Lord's work and go with your heart. Many major decisions that involve change, spending a lot of money, building a new addition to the church, and that requires any kind of church action will be divisive, and you will lose some people. You have to decide what is best for the Lord's work.

You can also decide to let the leadership of the church work it out. You can try to remain neutral and out of the middle of it. You can maintain your calling is to preach, witness, serve, and you will be on the frontline of ministry and service whatever direction the church takes. You will have naysayers who may say, "You aren't a leader." These will be the ones who want you to take a side, as long as it is their side. That is where you have to do as you feel God is leading you and not be coerced into being the "heavy", or the "hired gun", or simply just being used by a group of people who want to get their way concerning an issue in the church.

Chapter 13

Your Preaching/Teaching Style

Normally, ministers develop a preaching/teaching style. That usually comes after years of trial, error, success, a few failures, and a few bloopers as well.

I have preached plenty of bloopers. Most of us have. If you preach enough sermons, you are bound to lay a few eggs. It seems like those eggs roll off the platform and follow you back to the house. When you preach one, and you know it was terrible, it is hard to get it off your mind. Often, you try so hard to do better the next time that you come up with a message that ends up being better than average.

In pastoral ministry, you will have many opportunities to preach or teach. An occasional mediocre sermon is going to happen. Many pastors get into a rhythm of preaching "fairly" good sermons and get by with "fairly" good. When you are preaching two or three sermons a week, and if you can be "fairly" good each time you step up to the plate, then you are probably having a successful preaching/teaching ministry. Preaching "fairly" good all the time is better than preaching bad all the time.

A baseball player who hits a single almost every game is very valuable. The consistency of getting on base means that a run might score for the team. The home run hitters are very valuable, exciting, and needed. Often, they are the ones who drive the person on first base on to home plate. The minister who hits a lot of singles has a better chance of reaching home plate occasionally than the minister who goes to the pulpit and literally strikes out almost every time. Striking out happens occasionally in ministry. Often, it is because we did not study. We spent all our time visiting the hospitals and the grieving. We spent too much time trying to visit everybody and shake everybody's hand in the community. Or it was something that deflected us from our priority of studying. Often the problems and crises of our personal lives deplete us and keep us from reading and studying God's word. That will show up in our preaching.

You may be a homerun preacher. It could be that every time you step into the pulpit, you have something to deliver. You have prayed, studied, prepared, spiritually worked through any life issues or entanglements that might thwart a good message, and then just knocked that sermon right out of the park. That is where you would like to be, right? Don't you want to be that kind of preacher/teacher most of the time? When do you really want to stand up and speak and just strike at the ball and never hit the ball?

When I was a kid playing summer baseball, I had a season where I struck out almost every game. I could not hit a baseball with a snow shovel. I kept working on it and stayed with it. The next summer, I hit a lot of home runs and had a lot of base hits. It was a great turn around. It was more fun to hit home runs and base hits than it was to strikeout. It is more fun for the spectators too.

When you step up to speak, it is more fun to hit the ball out of the park or to at least get on base. In preaching, you can do it almost every time if you have spent time with God.

I am not talking about thunder and lightning. I am not talking about putting on a dramatic show for your congregation. That is about delivering the message. That is about having something to say and saying it understandably so that it goes down deep into the people's hearts. People should not leave the building wondering, "What did he or she say?" "What was that preacher talking about?" They should leave thinking about their wonderful Savior Jesus, and how they might be more like him and apply your message to their everyday living.

Let's face the facts, we know that people need the Lord. There is not one human on this planet whose life cannot be benefited, blessed, and made outright better by Jesus. People do not know this until they develop a love relationship with him. If you don't believe this, then you need to resolve it quickly or you will never preach a convincing message. If you don't think people need Jesus more than anything, you won't be hitting any home runs and probably never get on base. If you are in the ministry to stand in front of people and be seen, then you should get into theatre, politics, or show business. There are lots of places where you can show yourself to people. If you don't have a burden for people to come to know Jesus as Savior and Lord and believe they will spend eternity in hell without Jesus you aren't going to do very good in the ministry. Reconcile this immediately, or you are going to be very unfulfilled.

"He that goeth forth and weepeth, bearing precious seed, shall doubtless come again with rejoicing, bringing his sheaves with him." Psalm 126:6 is about the person who has a burden for other people. A person who cares enough to pray, and to weep for the souls of other people. A person who sows the seeds of the gospel. This person will be successful in seeing souls saved as the reward for the labor.

When I was a young boy, I went to church with my parents. They were United Baptists. United Baptists are not a very big group, but there are several of them in the mountains of East, Kentucky. There are quite a few where I am from in Martin county. They are good people. My mom and dad and grandparents were good United Baptists. My dad was baptized in a Freewill Baptist Church and then switched over to the United Baptists. I was never impressed much with the United Baptist preachers. As a child, I could never understand much of anything they said. All I heard and saw was a lot of deep breathing, gasping, hacking and facial contortions when they preached. It was very overwhelming for a child. Most of the ones I heard were good old boys who loved preaching, and I am sure they loved God and loved the Bible. They certainly did not explain or teach the Bible very well, but I am confident that they all held the Bible in high esteem.

By the time I was 12 years old, I begged my mom and dad to let me stay home from church. I couldn't stand church. Normally, it was always two hours long or longer. It was boring and very hard to understand what was going on. That should never happen in a worship service. If it is going to be boring, then keep it short. Do not bore people for a long time. If you don't have anything understandable to communicate, then it is best not to have anything at all. People's time is very precious, and there should be something worth hearing. I do believe some of the United Baptist ministers have worked hard and have come a long way. I have friends I grew up with who are now serving as United Baptist ministers, and I believe some are working hard to do a better job. Like all denominations, I do not agree with them on different beliefs. That is how it is when we compare different doctrines and denominations.

Growing up, I was exposed to a lot of preaching styles. My pastor, Jimmy Grayson, was a graduate of Carson Newman College in Tennessee and Southeastern Theological Seminary in North Carolina. He was a smart man. He did well in school. He was different from most of the preachers in our area. He presented sermons that were informing. He studied well. He prepared. He was articulate. He didn't act ignorant when he presented a sermon. He didn't come to the pulpit to put on a show. He had a dignity about him and fit in well with the First Baptist Church of Inez, Kentucky. Brother Jimmy, as we called him, never came unprepared, and he had something to say. He was my first encounter with a minister who I could understand. Brother Jimmy communicated on a level that children to adults could understand and enjoy. He was an excellent expositional preacher and teacher of the scriptures. He had a good background in New Testament Greek studies and often tied the Greek understanding of a word or text into his preaching. He occasionally stepped from behind the pulpit to make a point. Sometimes he would walk from side to side, but typically he stayed behind the pulpit. We did not have a microphone in the church because we were small. He always had to speak loud and articulate. Growing up, I thought that not using a microphone was a trademark of a good preacher. Eventually, I realized that it would be difficult in large groups.

Brother Grayson mentored me, reached out to me, and loved me as a young Christian and teenage preacher. His patience, love, forgiveness, and encouragement toward me seemed to be endless. When you are young, and someone is this good to you, you start thinking that this is normal. Soon, you learn that it is not. The harsh reality is that if there is anyone in your life who loves you with patience, forgiveness, and encouragement, you should value, cherish, and respect the individual. That is not how everyone in life and the ministry will treat you.

There were so many different ministers who I was around growing up. One young preacher came to our church often. He was over the top in his presentation. He would jump off the platform, pound on the pulpit, holler, and dress like he was a model for a magazine. Dynamic would be an understatement.

Many ministers who came were more subdued and often presented a 25-minute sermon with a text, three points, and a story or two at the end. I heard all of these types and most all of them were very good.

One preacher told story after story. Actually, he told too many stories. He was a well-loved and respected man, but all he did was tell stories. That grew a little wearisome.

As a preacher/teacher, you will have to develop your style of preaching. Your style will likely change the more you preach. Your style and the way you present your message will vary with the occasion, your audience, and the setting of the sermon.

When I was younger, I often thought there was a certain way I had to present my sermon. Eventually, you learn that you have to wait and see how God leads you to preach the sermon. Often, you do not know how you are going to deliver until you arrive and feel the atmosphere, see the crowd, and feel the vibe in the room. Sometimes the Holy Spirit will lead you to pull back and speak very quietly, reservedly, and calmly. There are occasions when you stand up, and you know it's an occasion where you can cut loose, talk loudly, and be a little more charismatic in your presentation. The main thing is, do not push a style that is uncomfortable or inappropriate for you. The worst style any of us can try to adopt is a style that is not us. Do not try to be somebody else. Be yourself. Often, we do not know who that it is when we are getting started. I loved Billy Graham and heard him several times. I watched him preach a lot on television. I wanted to preach like Billy Graham, and who didn't? He was the preacher of preachers and preached to masses of people. And, if you preach a little like Billy Graham, that is okay. There is nothing wrong with modeling him.

I thought Bob Russell from Southeast Christian Church, Louisville, Kentucky, did an excellent job. He handled a manuscript well. He read well. Some people cannot preach from a manuscript because they sound like they are reading their sermon, and they are. Bob Russell, could read his sermon, but you didn't mind, because his presentation was very interesting.

I listened to a lot of Adrian Roger's sermons as a younger adult. I haven't in a long time. In the past, I listened to so many of his sermons, that I almost always know when I hear someone preaching one of them. He was the prince of presenting and communicating. He was articulate. He had a booming voice. He could masterfully explain a text of scripture, always providing four of five points that began with the same letter. That is called alliteration. For example, long, lasting, Lord, love, life, little. Or, hurt, help, hope, heaven. A lot of ministers still do this today to guide them in presenting their text, and it can work well. The problem comes when you lock yourself into an alliteration, and then you can't come up with the one word that you need to go with the other three are using. It is a good presentation model, but don't lock yourself into this pattern. You will find it is better to come up with three or four points or words that convey want you are trying to communicate rather than to get hung up or stuck in an alliteration pattern.

Again, you will grow in your teaching and your preaching style the more you do it. Doing it more and more will make you better. Practice may not make you perfect, but practice, practice, and practice will make you much, much better. That is why you should never shy away from teaching or preaching in small, rural, urban, or wherever settings. Wherever you preach or teach, you are doing what you feel called to do, and you are putting your calling into practice. Whether it is in nursing homes, jails, Sunday school classes, small groups, or wherever. Especially starting out, you will preach where nobody else wants to preach. You will grow and develop and have more opportunities. The old saying is, blossom where you are planted and you will be transplanted.

When I was a teenager, I would preach in an old cemetery where my great grandfathers are buried. It is literally on top of an East, Kentucky mountain, up behind the house, where I grew up. I would walk up there, and there was no one to be seen or heard, just the graves. I would preach a big sermon. There was never a sound. No one looked at his or her cell phone. I did not do that a lot, but a few times. I have gone into empty sanctuaries and preached, even in little churches, where I started out pastoring. I would sometimes go when no one was around and get behind the pulpit to go through a message that I had on my mind. I have stood in the bathroom on occasion and gone through a message. There have been numerous other places too. Often, sitting at a desk or a table writing down notes, I have mentally rehearsed the message that I had on my mind. I felt embarrassed one time when a church lady walked into the sanctuary while I was preaching to the empty pews. I immediately excused myself and left the sanctuary. I was about 24 years old. Looking back, practicing, and rehearsing my notes, and my delivery was a good thing. It would have been better if I had done it more.

The musician practices for hours on end, in solitude. The athlete runs for miles alone. The businessman spends hours pondering, calculating, and working behind the scenes to make his business work. The preacher should spend hours improving his delivery and going over his or her message, burning it deep within the heart to deliver it with ease, unction, conviction, and passion.

A passionate sermon does not mean a loud sermon. Some of the most passionate sermons I have heard came from preachers who did not have to yell or scream. They changed the tone of their voices throughout the message. They paused and emphasized where necessary, but they did not have to try to stir up a storm hollering and making a lot of noise. Too many preachers make a lot of noise and never say anything. For sure, I am not against speaking loudly and have done so in a lot of my sermons. We just need to let the Holy Spirit do his work. If we are spiritually, mentally, physically ready, God is always ready.

Jesus is our example. He preached and taught as he had the opportunity. I would have loved to have sat with Jesus somewhere around the Sea of Galilee and listened to him. I would have loved hearing Jesus say anything. Can you imagine hearing his teaching about prayer or about not being judgmental? Watching Jesus do any of the miracles he performed or having a meal with him of any kind would have been so amazing. I know I would not have wanted to be at the cross when they crucified Jesus. I would not have wanted to have been near where they humiliated, abused him, and killed him on that cross. The disciples did not want to be there either. Peter was afraid to even acknowledge that he knew Jesus. So, I must realize that I am no better than any of the disciples. I couldn't have handled the agony of witnessing any human being treated that way. Sadly, none of us could have stopped it, or it would have been stopped, over 2,000 years ago. The plan was for Jesus to die for you and for me. He died for our sins. He became the sacrificial lamb of God who came to die, to give his blood to take away the sins of the world.1 John 2:2, says "He is the atoning sacrifice for our sins, and not only for ours but also for the sins of the whole world."

Spend some time studying the messages of Jesus and look at the settings where he spoke. Let's use Matthew's gospel as an example. Here is a list of sermons Jesus preached, as recorded by Matthew. You can also find a list in Mark, Luke, and John. These are here for illustration purposes. That would even be a good series for you preaching the sermons that Jesus preached.

Sermon on the Mount, Matthew 5: 1-7:29.
The Commissioning of the 12, Matthew 10: 1-42
John the Baptist, Matthew 11: 2-30
A house divided, Mathew 12:22-50
Parables by the Sea, Matthew 13: 1-53
Kingdom Greatness, Matthew 18:1-35
Authority of Christ, Matthew 21: 23-22:14
Woes to Leaders, Matthew 23: 1-39
The End of Time, Matthew 24: 1-26:2
The Upper Room Discourse, Matthew 26:26-35

When you study the sermons of Jesus, we learn how he preached. The way Jesus preached is a good way for us to preach. Jesus used memorable sayings. He would say things like, "Judge not, and you will not be judged; condemn not, and you will not be condemned; forgive and you will be forgiven; give and it will be given to you" Luke 6: 37-38. Jesus gave The Golden Rule which is a memorable saying, "So in everything, do to others what you would have them do to you, for this sums up the Law and the Prophets," Matthew 7:12 Normally, we say, do unto others as you would have them do unto you. When you preach, make your main point easy to remember. Figure out first what your point is and communicate your point. Use scripture, stories, and current events to communicate your point.

Jesus would use vivid imagery. He taught using outrageous examples. They were meant to get the point across, but were not meant to be taken literally. In Matthew 5: 29-30 Jesus did not mean that we should literally rip out our eyes and cut off our hands if we sin. If we took these words literally, Christians would be walking around blind and without hands. In Matthew 7: 3-5 he didn't mean that we literally have logs in our eyes, when we have been judgmental. He was making a point. Jesus said things that shocked people. He would use vivid imagery to shock people and to get his point across. Keep in mind Jesus was good at this. We have to be careful about using illustrations or saying things to shock people. I have used stories and repeated illustrations in the past that were a bit edgy or too shocking. Looking back, I wish I hadn't used them. As a young minister, I succumbed a few times to repeating newsy stories that simply contained too much shocking information. I now realize that too much information was not necessary. When we are young, we are often adventuresome, and while creativity is good, there should be boundaries. I never used an illustration or story that was incorrect or did not tie into the message, but I would not be comfortable repeating a few of them today. I suppose this comes a bit with aging.

Jesus also used repetition. Jesus spoke of his death and resurrection over and over again, Mark 8:31, 9:31; 10:33-34. Even with the repetition, the disciples still did not understand. However, find the main point of your sermon and say it again and again and illustrate it in different ways. I have heard preachers criticized for preaching an hour and repeating themselves over and over. That is not good. Preach your theme, use scripture, and illustrate your point or points in different ways and wrap it up in 30 minutes or less. On occasion, you can preach longer, but if you are preaching to the same people every week, less time over the long haul is better than long sermons.

Jesus also used object lessons. In Mark 12:41-44, he described unselfish giving after watching a widow drop two coins into an offering plate. In Matthew 18:1-4, he called a little child to him to talk about childlike faith. In John chapter 13: 3-17, he washed the feet of the disciples to teach servant leadership. When he told the parable of the sower, he was probably standing near a field. Visually communicated truth is powerful. From every day, there will come current event news stories you can use to illustrate your message. Spend some time perusing the news stories of the week, and you will find numerous stories that will serve as object lessons. If you want to preach like Jesus, use object lessons.

When Jesus preached, he told stories. He told parables. He connected everyday stories to make his messages memorable and understandable. Jesus told the story of the Prodigal son from Luke chapter 15 to teach us that God loves us, no matter how far we have wandered away. A sermon series based on the parables of Jesus will be a delightful study time for you and your people.

If you want to be a good preacher/teacher it will require time, practice, discipline, and patience. It is a growth process. I know I am a better preacher today than I was 40 years ago. I know I am better because I know me. People who knew me when I was a young adult might not think I am as good now as I was then. However, I feel I am better in my heart because I have grown as a person, a preacher, and in my walk with God. All of us should feel that time and aging have made us or will make us better. It would be tragic if we felt we had become worse.

Spend time alone with Jesus. Spend time preaching, just for Jesus. Go over your message and practice it some and see how the Lord likes it. If Jesus approves, then you are good to go to preach it to others. Spend a lot of time in prayer, reading, and preparing. Spend time early in the day with Jesus and preach like Jesus.

Chapter 14

Funerals

The minister will be called upon to participate in funerals. In most cases, you will have spent time with the person leading up to their death but not always. Once, I was asked, by a funeral director, to come to the cemetery to read the 23rd Psalm for someone I had never met. No one was there except the funeral director. The man had no family or anyone who cared to be there. I read the 23rd Psalm and had a prayer. Occasionally situations like this occur.

The most common situation is that I have usually known the person and spent many hours with the individual leading up to his or her death. Typically, visits in the hospital, or the home have been a regular occurrence leading up to the time of death, the day of the funeral visitation, the funeral, and the burial.

The pastor of the church or any minister associated with the church staff has the opportunity to utilize every ministerial gift that he or she has in this setting. I have preached or participated, in some way, in hundreds of funeral sermons.

You will have many opportunities to help people transition from this life to the next. The Bible speaks of the valley of the shadow of death. There is a valley that we walk through from this life to the next. Death often happens suddenly with no warning. Often death is a very slow, day by day or even week by week process. Someone may be ill for many months in a nursing home facility. The minister brings the message and comfort of God's love and grace. The minister brings Jesus and eternal life into the conversation. He talks about what is ahead and how the Lord our Shepherd will lead us there. His angels will protect us and guide us on the journey. God will take care of all that we need, and his provisions for us will be abundant. There will be no poverty, no sickness, no worries, no loneliness, no pain or disease in heaven. Heaven is to be looked forward to as a place of joy, peace, and happiness. The minister works closely with the sick and the dying to bring assurance of great treasures that await the believer in Christ on the other side of death.

Often, the minister will have the opportunity to help someone pray to receive Christ as Lord and personal Savior. If we are unsure, we should all ask the question, "Have you prayed and asked Jesus to be your personal Savior?" Do not ever take for granted that someone has unless you have known the person for some time and heard their testimony of knowing Christ as Lord and Savior. Do not assume anything.

When it is time for the funeral, the greatest comfort you can give the family is to be able to say that you know by the testimony and life of the deceased that he or she is with the Lord and being well cared for. Sad indeed is the funeral where everybody leaves with uncertainty concerning the individual's eternal destination.

During the time of sickness and grief, you help the dying to walk through a time of prayer. That is the time that you talk about God's grace, love, and forgiveness. All have sinned.

Some of the finest Christian people I know spend the last weeks of life very worried about all the mistakes they have made in life. Even the finest Christians begin to worry that God will hold these sins against them. They worry that maybe they haven't lived a good enough life. Suddenly the simplicity of the gospel message becomes fuzzy. Some wonder, "Is believing in Jesus enough?" And, "Have I really believed in Jesus?" "Have I truly repented of my sins, and has God really forgiven me?" The minister has the unique opportunity to help the sick and dying answer these very important questions. Most important, is leading the sick in times of prayer, where the individual can silently say anything they need to say to God. They might want to pray out loud just between the two of you. You definitely do not want any family or friends around during this time. That is between the person and God with you as the helper or leader in prayer. Or, they may pray a prayer silently as you lead in the prayer where they have the opportunity to ask for forgiveness, to repent of sin, and to reaffirm their acceptance of Jesus and love for him. For the dying to say or simply affirm, "Lord, I want to be with you in heaven," will be a time of assurance and spiritual strength during the walk through death's valley.

During this time, the minister is a Christian witness to the family and friends who gather. You will shake hands and receive hugs from loved ones. They will see you as their point of contact with God. You will be Jesus to them in these hours of grief and loss. Sometimes you can say too much. Some ministers never learn to control their tongues and ramble on as if everybody wants to hear them talk nonstop. Be comforting. Be helpful. Offer words of assurance about your time and prayers with the loved one. Let them know that you know they are at peace with God. You have prayed with them, and you have heard their testimony. You can relay this to the family to help them in their time of grief. During this time, family members may want to hear more about the message of Christ. If they are not interested, hopefully, there will be later occasions for you to share with them the Christian message.

The funeral will certainly be the occasion where you can talk about Heaven and the importance of preparing for their destinies. Emphasize that if they want to see their loved one again, they should be sure that Jesus is in their hearts as Lord and Savior. As the loved one is deceased, your job is to help the family to reflect, remember, and hopefully celebrate the person's life and homegoing to be with the Lord. Your message must help them find and experience comfort. As they leave the funeral, your message should provide some sense of peace and direction for life.

That is a tall order, but it will be a major accomplishment if you are successful. To some degree, you will have some success and also some failure. Some people will tune you out, and there will be those who will give you their utmost attention. However, your job is not necessarily to be successful but to be faithful in delivering the message and allowing God to work through you.

You can't snap your fingers and change people or the situation of the deceased. Some folks want the minister to walk in and make everything beautiful for everyone. That seldom happens. You can be compassionate, empathetic, and deliver God's message of love, grace, and hope. Say what you know to be true, and never fabricate anything. If you knew the person, this helps a lot. If you did not know the person, then you have to rely on what you have been told. Do the best you can and hopefully you can establish some rapport with those who are there.

In every audience, some people need the Lord, a church home, and a pastor. In a funeral service, you have the golden opportunity to present Jesus, be an advertisement for your church, and be the minister God has called you to be.

Funerals do not have to be long or short. To me, short funerals are the saddest because there does not seem to be much to say. Or, no one wants to spend much time at a service remembering the deceased. Most ministers will hear this often in their lifetime, "We want the service to be brief." Seldom do people say they want a long service. However, I have been in funeral services that were almost three hours long. I wondered in those funerals if they thought they could bring the dead back to life.

There should be a balance when it comes to the length of a funeral service. The deceased's life is now finished. Take a little time and reflect on this person. Let the family memorialize the deceased if they will. Encourage them to exhibit photographs, reflect on his or her accomplishments, their interests, and what made that person a special human being who will be missed by the world. Point out what you will miss about the deceased and what the family and friends will miss about the deceased. The funeral is the time to forget the bad if there is any. Hopefully, it was forgotten long before the funeral, and all peace was made between friends and family months or years before death. The funeral is the time to celebrate the individual's life and their eternal homegoing, where all in Christ will be together again. It does not need to be two hours long, but 15 minutes is extremely short. There have been occasions when I have stood at the cemetery, it was about five degrees with snow on the ground, and the wind was blowing. Fifteen minutes in those conditions seemed like an eternity.

Every situation is different. Talk closely with the family and work together to have a funeral ceremony that no one is ashamed to remember. The minister always does his or her best. You prepare, you study the person's life, you know them from spending time with them, and then you do all you can to comfort and encourage those who are in attendance. It is not always easy. Often, there are hurdles with funerals. The time of year, weather, families who may be divided and not working together are never easy. You do the best you can do and trust God for the rest.

The scriptures you will use at the funeral service may vary because people are different, and the Bible is a big book with a lot of scriptures. The 23rd Psalm has probably been read more than any passage at a funeral or graveside service. The King

James Version is certainly the most popular since that is what most people have heard throughout their lives.

23 The Lord is my shepherd; I shall not want. [2]He maketh me to lie down in green pastures: he leadeth me beside the still waters. [3]He restoreth my soul: he leadeth me in the paths of righteousness for his name's sake. [4]Yea, though I walk through the valley of the shadow of death, I will fear no evil: for thou art with me; thy rod and thy staff they comfort me. [5]Thou preparest a table before me in the presence of mine enemies: thou anointest my head with oil; my cup runneth over. [6]Surely goodness and mercy shall follow me all the days of my life: and I will dwell in the house of the Lord for ever."

Another passage that I have read at many funerals is from John 14: 1-6. "14 Let not your heart be troubled: ye believe in God, believe also in me. [2]In my Father's house are many mansions: if it were not so, I would have told you. I go to prepare a place for you. [3]And if I go and prepare a place for you, I will come again, and receive you unto myself; that where I am, there ye may be also. [4]And whither I go ye know, and the way ye know. [5]Thomas saith unto him, Lord, we know not whither thou goest; and how can we know the way? [6]Jesus saith unto him, I am the way, the truth, and the life: no man cometh unto the Father, but by me."

That is a passage of God's comfort. You are pointing out that Jesus has prepared a place for the departed. That place is a good place because Jesus is there. Wherever Jesus is, is a good place. Jesus has prepared the place, and it has to be a good place.

How does a person go to this wonderful place that Jesus has prepared? Jesus said to the disciples, "I am the way, the truth, and the life: no man cometh unto the Father, but by me." All who have trusted in Christ for their salvation look forward to the wonderful place that Jesus has prepared.

Another favorite scripture of many ministers is 2nd Corinthians chapter 5:1-9. "For we know that if the earthly tent we live in is destroyed, we have a building from God, an eternal house in heaven, not built by human hands. [2]Meanwhile we groan, longing to be clothed instead with our heavenly dwelling, [3]because when we are clothed, we will not be found naked. [4]For while we are in this tent, we groan and are burdened, because we do not wish to be unclothed but to be clothed instead with our heavenly dwelling so that what is mortal may be swallowed up by life. [5]Now the one who has fashioned us for this very purpose is God, who has given us the Spirit as a deposit, guaranteeing what is to come. [6]Therefore we are always confident and know that as long as we are at home in the body we are away from the Lord. [7]For we live by faith, not by sight. [8]We are confident, I say, and would prefer to be away from the body and at home with the Lord. [9]So we make it our goal to please him, whether we are at home in the body or away from it."

The point to be made from this scripture is that the departed loved one has not only departed the body but is now home with the Lord. Absent from the body is present with the Lord. The body no longer contains our loved one. They have left the body, and are now clothed with their heavenly dwelling.

Another popular scripture is 1st Corinthians 13. The entire chapter is beautiful and is read at many weddings. However, verse 12 is a comforting verse of scripture for funerals.

1 Corinthians 13:12 "12 For now, we see only a reflection as in a mirror; then we shall see face to face. Now I know in part; then I shall know fully, even as I am fully known. The apostle Paul looks forward to the day when we shall know each other in heaven. "Then I shall know fully, even as I am fully known." When we get to heaven, we will recognize each other and understand each other. "Now we know in part, then I shall know fully, even as I am fully known." In this life, a lot of our problems hinge on our inability to understand each other. Then, we shall know fully, even as I am fully known, the scripture says.

Psalm 90:12-17 "12 So teach us to number our days, that we may apply our hearts unto wisdom." This verse reminds us all that life is not forever. We have a specific number of days. A 100-year life still has a specific number of days, as does the brief life of a child. All life, in reality, is very brief. What has happened to the deceased person, happens to us all. All of us come to that point and place in life. We all should prepare for this event.

There are many scriptures that you will turn to in the hours leading up to death and during the service for the deceased. Family members will sometimes recommend verses they want you to read that are personal to them. Sadly, we are living in a day where many people are more and more unfamiliar with the Bible. Families will look to you in most cases to provide the scripture and to direct them through this wilderness journey of death and closure.

The funeral is the time for all ministers to utilize the utmost patience. This is not about the minister. This event is about helping the family and showing the greatest respect and honor possible for them and the deceased. You are there to help in any way possible.

One decision you will have to work out within yourself and with your church family is this-will you be expected to officiate funerals on your day off? I have only known one minister who never eulogized or preached a funeral on his day off, and he pulled it off. He was upfront about it. His day off was for spending time with his family. He always took that day off. It worked for him.

Many ministers never think of this until the water is under the bridge, and they cannot do anything about it. Once you start being available for every whim, every call, any time of day, then it seems like you become stuck in this rut. In ministry, this one reason so many ministers and families simply burn out. Your spouse or children are looking forward to a day at the lake, and it has to be canceled because of a funeral. I have found most funeral directors like to determine the date of the funeral, and they always prefer to have them at the funeral home because it is convenient for them.

Sit down with your leadership and simply say, my spouse, my children, and I deserve one day a week that is ours, and then stick to it. Eventually, your congregation will set the funeral director straight. If your day off is Tuesday or Friday or whenever, when it comes time for them to set a date for the funeral and they want you to show up, then they will say to the funeral director, "It cannot be Tuesday, because that is our pastor's day off." Funerals can be held on Monday or Wednesday. That is something I never really thought about but sorely wish I had earlier in my ministry. If you are in an active church ministry, do all you can to protect a day a week for you and your family to do family things.

Funeral ministry is a constant ministry of the pastor. Whether you have a small congregation or large one, there is seldom a week that your ministry services are not required to lead, to help, to comfort the sick and the dying, and then those left behind. Use these moments as great opportunities to let the love of God in Jesus shine through your life to make a difference. Your reward will be the difference you make in the lives of others for the sake of Jesus and his glory.

Chapter 15

Weddings

"Husbands, love your wives, just as Christ loved the church and gave himself up for her," Ephesians 5:2

"Be completely humble and gentle; be patient, bearing with one another in love.3 Make every effort to keep the unity of the Spirit through the bond of peace," Ephesians 4: 2-3

"But Ruth replied, "Don't urge me to leave you or to turn back from you. Where you go, I will go, and where you stay, I will stay. Your people will be my people and your God my God. [17]Where you die I will die, and there I will be buried. May the Lord deal with me, be it ever so severely, if even death separates you and me." Ruth 1: 16-17

"So God created mankind in his own image in the image of God he created them; male and female he created them. [28]God blessed them and said to them, "Be fruitful and increase in number; fill the earth and subdue it. Rule over the fish in the sea and the birds in the sky and over every living creature that moves on the ground." Genesis 1: 27-28

"That is why a man leaves his father and mother and is united to his wife, and they become one flesh." Genesis 2:24

"Two are better than one, because they have a good return for their labor:" Ecclesiastes 4:9

"Be devoted to one another in love. Honor one another above yourselves," Romans 12:10

"Be kind and compassionate to one another, forgiving each other, just as in Christ God forgave you." Ephesians 4:32

"My beloved is mine and I am his," Song of Solomon 2:16

"Many waters cannot quench love;rivers cannot sweep it away." Song of Solomon 8:7

"So they are no longer two, but one flesh. Therefore what God has joined together, let no one separate." Matthew 19:6

"My command is this: Love each other as I have loved you," John 15:12

You will have multiple opportunities to perform weddings. When you serve in ministry positions, you will get to know people who will want you to officiate their marriage ceremonies, and sign the licenses that they receive at the local county court clerk's office. That may be a different office in other countries.

When I was 18, I obtained my first wedding license. I had just been ordained, and my father had to go to the courthouse to sign a $500 bond. Laws are always changing. Today you may only need to show your certificate or ordination to the clerk at the courthouse. Always check out the rules for your state and your country. Whatever the rules are, you will often be completing the paperwork for a legal document. You will need to strictly adhere to the rules of the state or country where you reside.

You do not have to perform wedding ceremonies, unless, you are promoting yourself as a community wedding officiant. There are resort areas in the United States such as Las Vegas, Nevada, Gatlinburg, Tennessee, and various other places where a lot of wedding chapels exist, and a lot of people make careers of officiating weddings. An alumnus of our school went to work in Pigeon Forge, Tennessee, for a wedding chapel and was overwhelmingly busy officiating weddings.

You can be busy in almost any community you live in listening to people's wedding vows, helping them orchestrate their ceremony, signing their documents, and working with them to prepare for their wedding ceremony.

In some cases, you can do as much as you want or as little as you want, with wedding ceremonies. Some ministers spend hours with a couple involved in the planning of the wedding. Some couples want a wedding planner who will do all the planning, but only want the minister for the actual officiation. I have done both. I have spent hours and hours with couples working with them up to the moment of pronouncing them man and wife and then usually attended some of the reception that followed the ceremony. That will be up to you and how much you want to do with wedding ceremonies.

Conducting ceremonies can be a good ministry. You can meet people, help people, get to know them better and be a very integral part of their lives. People will always remember you for the time that you took to help them through one of the most special and sacred moments of their lives. For years to come, they may call upon you in times of sickness and even death to stand with them. Some of these people will be involved in your ministry and support your church. Some people, you will never see again. To some, you are simply a person who can legally sign their marriage document. They may even hope, to never see you again.

When it comes to weddings, you have to mentally and spiritually prepare yourself for the role that you want to fill. You have to set your limits, or people will be telling you what, when, and how you are going to do everything. That will eventually become tiresome. It is better to come up with a plan for handling weddings and then stick to your plan. For example, there may be scenarios or situations that you do not want to officiate, and you should not do it if it goes against your convictions. There can be a myriad of different reasons depending on the situation. Attorneys do not take every case presented to them. A surgeon does not do every surgical procedure for everyone who walks in the door. People are often referred to someone else. There may be cases where you will feel better to refer a couple to someone else. That will be your call. You have to understand that it is okay if people are inconvenienced, and even a little disappointed.

I only regret participating in a few wedding ceremonies. I have done hundreds. A couple of times, a couple slid too much music into the ceremony that was inappropriate for a church wedding. I remember thinking, "How did this happen?"

Wedding ceremonies will be up to you and the couple you are marrying. There are many wedding ceremonies you can find on the Internet that you can edit and use for different occasions. A wedding ceremony can be as long or as short as you want it to be. They can sing to each other, make speeches to each other, light candles, have communion, have various prayers, speak to the audience, and have people participate in all sorts of ways. When it comes to a church or Christian wedding, there should be dignity, sacredness, and boundaries. People can still laugh, and funny things can take place if that is what the couple wants. Yet, the essence of the ceremony should have the feeling that Jesus is present, and this marriage is about pleasing him, involving him not only in the ceremony but in all the lives represented at the wedding.

The wedding is about the couple, but it proclaims a message to all who are attending. Statements made by the minister. Symbolism carried out at the wedding. How you and the wedding party conduct yourselves will be remembered by those attending for a lifetime. People do not forget about weddings. They especially remember any foul-ups or anything that did not go smoothly.

A friend of mine was conducting a small wedding, and the altar table behind him caught on fire. He was videotaped, putting out the fire. It ended up on television's America's Funniest Home Videos and has been seen by millions. It is hilarious. Fortunately, he and the couple put out the fire and completed the ceremony. Those are the types of interruptions that you hope never happen, but anything can happen. It is good to talk about this when you are planning the ceremony. Advise the couple that if something goes wrong, the necessary time will be taken to regroup and keep the ceremony moving. You always hope there will not be any interruptions and that the important people show up. In this day and time, almost anything can happen. You are smart to try to think about it and have a plan as to how you will handle the scenario. The bigger the wedding, the more opportunities there are for something to be forgotten, someone like the best man is late, forgets to show up, or some intruder pops in to spoil the event. Always go over some of the "what ifs" and at least know, between you and the wedding party, that while you are going to plan for the perfect wedding, it is better to be prepared to make adjustments as necessary.

Weddings can involve a couple of days of your time. Many of them happen on Saturday with a Friday night rehearsal. That means you will need to study for Sunday accordingly if you are preaching or leading in any Sunday studies or events. Also, this will impact your family time. Be sure you take a day off to spend time doing something with your family. Weddings and funerals happen a lot in ministry. While you, your spouse, and family may attend, it is not family time for you.

Keep in mind that wedding ceremonies do not have to be long and ongoing. However, do not make them so short that they appear to be insignificant. Normally, the couple will tell you what they want. As the officiant, you have every right to say, "This is what I do when I perform a ceremony." You can lay out what you do. You may want to read scripture, have a time of prayer and say a few words to them and the audience about marriage. If they do not want you to do that, the couple should find someone else.

Ask about the music upfront. If you do not want to be the "bad" guy in saying no to some music that you deem distasteful, then you might want to have a wedding director in your church. She or he can make the decisions about some things like music, props, dress, or any details that you do not want to be involved in deciding. Hopefully, you and your wedding planner will have an understanding and agreement already set about wedding particulars. She or he can simply have a document that can give to the couple that outlines the guidelines for weddings.

It will be best for you if your ministry leadership approves this document. It is official when you can give this to someone saying, "These are the wedding guidelines for weddings taking place in our church." This will lay out what your church expects. This document should also include remuneration to the church, custodial persons, musicians, officiating minister, wedding coordinator, nursery staff, and any others. Keep the document simple. You do not need to scare the couple to death but, it is best for you, the church, and them if everyone understands the expectations in hopes that the wedding is a great event for everyone.

Chapter 16

Win Souls to Christ

Jesus came to seek and to save the lost, Luke 19:10. If he had not, you and I would be lost in our sins and unable to save ourselves from hell and an eternity separated from God. There is nothing worse than being lost and nothing more unimaginable than to be lost forever throughout eternity.

Before we were saved, we were lost. But, when we became saved, we were saved. Those of us who are saved, know the difference between being saved and being lost. There have certainly been times during my Christian pilgrimage that I have been prodigal, rebellious, carnal, sinful, worldly, and off the track in my relationship with God. Somehow, by his power, grace, and steadfast love, he has never turned me loose or let me fall from his strong hand. I rejoice that the love of God is greater than man. Jesus said in John 10:28-30, "And I give unto them eternal life; and they shall never perish, neither shall any man pluck them out of my hand. My Father, which gave them me, is greater than all; and no man is able to pluck them out of my Father's hand. I and my Father are one." And then, "God so loved the world that he gave his only begotten son that whosoever believeth in him shall not perish but hath eternal life," John 3:16.

Jesus came and willingly died on a cross to sacrifice himself for lost sinners. If you do not believe any of this, then you must step aside immediately and reconcile what you do believe. If the ministers in communities, villages, cities, and farmlands do not believe that people are lost, without Christ, then the work of Jesus is in peril. Fortunately, the work of Jesus has always had a group of believers who have proclaimed the good news of God's love, often with great sacrifice, to tell the story of Jesus so that others can know him and be saved.

There are many tasks you will be called upon to do in ministry. Sometimes you will feel like a community baby sitter. There will be people who will emotionally deplete you because they are constantly needing attention or making requests of you. Do not get bogged down, holding everybody's hands. There are times for this. There are the hours when you will be the only friend somebody has while they are dying in a hospital or nursing home. You may be the only person who will help or speak to the person who is released from jail. You may be the only one who shows any care or concern for the person who has just lost a spouse in death or divorce. You may be the only person who tries to help someone obtain a bag of groceries for their family. Many times you will be the only Jesus that so many will ever see or experience.

Keep in mind how Jesus loved the downtrodden and cared for and healed the sick. The ministry is not all about evangelism. While all ministry is a form of evangelism, it is not 24 hours of knocking on doors trying to get people to pray the sinner's prayer to receive Christ. The world would be better if we spent more time doing exactly that. We must win the lost and be very busy about winning the lost. Everything we do, whether it is feeding the hungry, clothing the poor, educating the community, counseling the hurting, or healing the sick, should be done with the outreaching hand of Jesus. On hearing this, Jesus said to them, "It is not the healthy who need a doctor, but the sick. I have not come to call the righteous, but sinners," Mark 2:17.

The sick are all around us. There is mental illness, spiritual darkness, poverty, ignorance, physical illness, and lostness. You do not have to think long about all the hurt that is on this planet. Every day, a billion people struggle for a decent drink of water. There is massive hunger on this planet. Sickness abounds around the world. Homelessness is seen around the world. Masses of people are unsure of how they are going to survive today. They cannot even think about tomorrow. You and I can help them. As ministers of the gospel, we are called to help them. We have an answer. We have a source of strength, direction, hope, help, recovery, encouragement, light, and safety. His name is Jesus. He is the way, the truth, and the life, John 14:6.

You and I, as well as all ministers and Christians across the globe, must tell people the good news of Jesus. We are recipients of his grace and mercy and should likewise share the message of hope to all. Our purpose is reaching people who are without Christ, not merely to grow church attendance, although it will. Reaching people should never be about increasing the financial gifts of the church, although it will. It should also never be about having the biggest church in town, although your church will be larger than most. Our purpose is to do what Jesus commanded us to do. He said, "Therefore go and make disciples of all nations, baptizing them in the name of the Father and of the Son and of the Holy Spirit," Matthew 28:19. However, when we do what Jesus told us to do, our ministries will be blessed. You cannot ignore soul winning and have a successful ministry.

A lot of people have a maintenance ministry. Often people will inherit what someone else has done, and they will maintain it for a few years. That is not completely negative. It is better to do a good job maintaining a ministry than killing a ministry. If you maintain a ministry you will keep families attending and at least baptize the children and grandchildren of those who are attending. That is the kind of ministry we see in many places. Every year, thousands of churches will baptize one or none. In my denomination, it is routine to hear reports of 6,000 or 7,000 churches who baptize one or none for an entire year. That is awful. The pastors and leaders should be winning and baptizing several people a year. If the pastor cannot lead one person to Christ all year, then what has the pastor done? Nothing. He has shown up. Preached a message of some kind and collected whatever pay he can confiscate from the church. I do not want to be overly harsh. I suppose there may be cases where there is not one lost person in the village or community to win to Christ. Of course, I have trouble believing this. If this is your situation, be patient and watchful as God will surely bring you into contact with someone soon who needs to be saved.

In most cases, if the minister has an ongoing awareness that people need the Lord, he or she will at least baptize a child or two. There will be a spouse of someone who will come to Christ. Someone will have a friend who needs the Lord. There will be someone who someone knows who is hurting and needs Christ. In most situations, unless you are serving a church on a planet where there is no life, you should be winning and baptizing a few people to Christ every year.

Liberty Baptist Church was my first pastoral opportunity. I was invited to preach for them when I was 16 years old. The church had all but closed but had one family in the church that had a vision of keeping it open. Harold and June Rice of Paintsville, Kentucky, believed God still had a work to perform in the small rural community of Denver, Kentucky. They decided to try to have church on the second and fourth Sundays of the month at 2:00 in the afternoon. I was invited to preach during my sophomore year of high school. We had the Rice family, which consisted of five people, their grandmother, and a couple of other people. After a few months, we were having 15 to 20 in attendance. The church officially called me as their pastor when I began my senior year of high school. By this time, the Elizabeth Jarrell Baptist Church in Louisa, Kentucky, also called me to be their pastor. Their services were held on Sunday morning. Their attendance averaged about 30 people. We had baptisms at both churches. Liberty had not had any baptisms for a long time. We did not have a baptistry at Liberty but a nice picturesque creek in front of the church where we had several baptisms. In my senior year of high school, June Rice and I spent a lot of weekday nights handing out gospel tracts and inviting people to church. The work that she and Harold and their family did and what God did through our available efforts brought new people to the church.

Wading in that creek, down to a greater depth of water, with a crowd of people standing on the bank, is quite a memory. There is something special about a summer baptism, in an open-air stream of water, with a crowd gathered singing Shall We Gather at the River. We did this numerous times. Today, Liberty Baptist has a beautiful country church facility. There is a four-lane highway that makes the church very accessible, and the church is very much alive. I was a green high school boy who knew very little. I knew about Jesus dying on the cross and that he was the way to be saved. I preached Jesus and faith in him, and the Lord added to that church new converts to Christ despite me. Thankfully, people overlooked the ignorance of my youth and were inspired by my youthful enthusiasm for Christ. The church became alive again. What seemed like an impossible place to grow and pastor a church became an attractive place to serve. Today, there is a fine church in Denver, Kentucky

Multiple baptisms took place in every church I ever served. I never served a church that did not grow. Forks of Elkhorn Baptist Church in Midway, Kentucky, had few baptisms in years before calling me as their pastor. Today, the church is in the middle of horse fields. However, it has a multimillion-dollar property and buildings with hundreds of people attending. Many years before, my place of service was bringing the church back from an attendance of 30 to over 100 and winning people to Christ. We baptized often. It seemed no one was around, but people did come, and people were saved and were added to the church. Years later, the church almost died again, but they came back, and today the church is one of the best and strongest in Kentucky.

Any place will do. God can do miracles anywhere. People can be saved in any community, or any place, if you have a heart and passion to win people to Christ.

Stamping Ground Baptist Church in Stamping Ground, Kentucky, had only a few baptisms or additions in the several years preceding my service there. After being there a few months, I was able to announce our 40th addition to the church, with over half of them being baptisms. For a little small redundant village church that was stagnant and dead, it was a great victory.

At First Baptist Church, Highland Heights, Kentucky, we led the association of churches in baptisms during my tenure. We often had 20 to 40 people who came out every Thursday night to go knocking on the doors of prospects. Our outreach program at Highland Heights was incredible. We had small group Sunday School classes in every nook and cranny of the church's facility. We even had partitions available for a small group Sunday School class. Our Sunday School program was phenomenal, and our people had a heart for reaching out and loving people. I cannot take credit for this because the church already had a passion to reach people before I got there. However, we did take it to another level with enthusiasm, baptisms, and further growth. The church became a place known for great fellowship, excitement, and an overall attractive place to attend church because of the positive fellowship we enjoyed.

While at First Baptist Church, Pikeville, Kentucky, we led the entire region in baptisms and church growth for over eight years. At Pikeville, we often had crowds between 600 and 700 on Sunday morning. We renovated downtown Pikeville. We bought and demolished the old city high school and made way for 120 extra parking spaces. We arranged for Hardee's restaurant to own the corner of the property and gained parking access to Hardees on Sunday morning. A city high school gym facility was also connected to the property, and we gained access to parking in this area for Sunday morning. It was a massive project, financially and mentally, for a church that was averaging less than 200 when I started there. While there, we renovated the sanctuary, which cost almost a half-million dollars in the mid-eighties. We became the first church to broadcast a 30-minute worship service on regional television and did so most of the eight years I was there. There was much growth in every area of the church.

Financially, we had miraculous Christmas for Christ offerings that went mostly for mission causes. One Sunday, every December, we would collect between $60,000 to over $80,000 in a single offering. In the late eighties and early nineties, this was a ton of money and would be a tremendous sum anytime. The people gave sacrificially. Most everyone, from those on limited incomes to those with tremendous incomes, participated in this offering. They were truly miracle offerings. In the early eighties, First Baptist Church Pikeville, Kentucky, was down in attendance and was a very depressing place. The area, with the dilapidated old high school out front, made it look like the church was in the slums of the community. The building was a painted cinder block sanctuary. It looked like something that had been started but never finished. The worship services were dead. It was a Sunday morning place for a small town and small crowd to gather. However, anyplace will do because God can do anything if he is allowed to work. We started an outreach program. Several of us went to visit people every week. We knocked on doors. We prayed for people to be saved. The gospel of Jesus was preached. Several of us in the church had a great burden for lost souls, and God did a great work of church growth at First Baptist Church, Pikeville. Kentucky.

Gateway Baptist Church in Newburgh, Indiana, was averaging small crowds when I went there in the early nineties. We grew from 50 to over 300. We baptized people routinely. We were one of the strongest and most vibrant churches in our region of Southern, Indiana. We built a beautiful new worship facility, and almost every Sunday, we had visitors and additions to our church. When I was called to Gateway, it was a place very few wanted to serve as pastor because attendance was down, and finances were very limited. God did a great work there. I served Gateway Baptist for ten years. We had large crowds. We were one of the most baptizing churches in our area. We completed a massive building program. We had strong offerings. We had more staff than at any time in the church's history. We paid the staff more than they had ever been paid. The church had enough money to pay all the bills without worries. We kept a constant stream of prospects and interested people coming to the church. People were interested in us. They came looking to join and to be involved. It was a phenomenal ten years of ministry, of winning lost souls to Jesus, of fellowship, and being an overall part of the Lord's exciting work.

We baptized so many people from all walks of life, from the aged to young professionals moving into our area. One weekend our baptistry heater went out, but we had a young doctor who wanted to be baptized. He insisted on going through with the baptism even though the water would be freezing cold. A deacon and I carried water from the kitchen on the other end of the building to help fill up that baptistry with some warmer water. It was an all-day project because the kitchen was about 75 yards away from the baptistry. We raised the temperature of the baptistry some. The young doctor was excited and rejoiced in following Jesus in baptism. His family became very faithful, in our church. I add this story to underscore that baptisms are important. Lost souls are important. We cared enough about that guy to carry water most of the day to pull off that baptism. At that time, our church had a heart and a burden for lost souls and baptizing people. Any place will do if you have a burden and a heart for reaching lost people for Jesus.

Some areas are often remote, and maybe a dozen or so baptisms a year is all you will have. However, in today's world, people will drive 30 miles to your church regardless of where it is if you are preaching good sermons and have a positive ministry going on. I have seen a lot of secluded, out of the way churches grow and baptize dozens of people. The gospel of Jesus is like a magnet that pulls people in. Jesus said in John 12:32, "And I, if I be lifted up from the earth, will draw all men unto me."

Any place will do when you bring God into a situation. Anything can happen because God can do anything.

I could write a lot more about the success of my previous church pastoral ministries. However, the point is not to tout me or pat myself on the back. I simply praise God for the opportunity to have served in so many churches where God blessed in such bountiful ways. My point is, almost every place, where I was called to, had challenges. The ministries became better, stronger, and more attractive attendance-wise as well as financially. God always seemed to show up and do miracles.

It all begins with your heart. Any ministry and place can do better if your burden is lost, souls. If you will win people to Jesus in your ministry, it will solve nearly every problem you have. It may not solve the nagging church member who is determined to make your life miserable. They can inflict a lot of pain on you and your family. However, if you are praying for lost souls and leading them to Christ, and the church is baptizing people, and you are growing some, then these people cannot hurt you as badly. Love covers a multitude of sins, so does leading people to Jesus.

Make a prayer list of people you want to win to Christ. That is especially important if you are early in your ministry at a church because you do not know many if any, people in a new community. Sit down with your leaders, deacons, or elders. Ask them for names of people who need to be saved. Some people will look at you strangely because some church members have not heard the words "saved" or "lost" before. If this happens to you, ask for the names of people who they would like to see join the church or who needs to join the church. Some people equate joining the church with salvation, which is not salvation. You have to start someplace. The main point is to start gathering names of people who you and the church are going to pray for, to be saved. Make this a team effort. Enlist others to be thinking about these people and praying for them to come to Christ.

Often, I used Wednesday night prayer services to enlarge our prayer list. I would ask for people to offer names of people that we could add to our prayer list. A long list or a short list is good. You are focusing on people. The work of the Lord is people. We are to be about winning people to Christ.

As you have the opportunity you want to try to meet as many of these people as possible. You have an in-road to them. Someone in your church knows them. You can call or approach them and say, "John Doe goes to our church, and he said he knew you and we all are interested in having you worship with us one Sunday." Or, if they have children or other needs, you can approach the prospect about how you hope to minister to them. They may have small children, and you may be able to offer a children's choir or other children's programs. They may have teenagers, and you may be able to encourage them to involve their teens in your teen program. Or, you may simply approach them and invite them to come and worship with you. Most people are not invited to church anymore. As of this writing, I have been invited to church one time in the last 20 years. I was so touched that I attended. I have been invited many times to speak to different churches. However, I have only been invited to a local pastor's church as a congregant-one time.

So many people are hungry for inclusion and friendship. You will be surprised how many people will show up if you invite them to stop by and visit. Do not pressure them. Let them know your heart would be thrilled anytime they might come and visit.

Make winning souls to Jesus a priority in your life and ministry. Jesus gave us the example. He cared for us. He told us to go and win others. That is what we are to be about. Be patient. Sow seeds. It does not happen overnight. Your ministry will see results when this becomes a part of your daily life.

One more word. You will have Sundays and even weeks when no one will publicly receive Christ. You may have months with no baptisms. You may have seasons when it seems there is no one around anywhere to reach with the gospel. Do not sweat this. God has not called you to be successful but to be faithful. Do the work that God has called you to do. Live for him. Do the ministry you are called to be doing at your church. Study, pray, disciple others, minister to others, be busy in service for the Lord for whatever that entails each day. Always be aware that people need the Lord. More often than not, you will have opportunities to tell others about Jesus and his love for them and the difference he makes in every life.

The Lord will give you souls for your labor.

Chapter 17

Control Your Tongue

There is much that a minister trains for through education and practice. Many have sheer talents that they bring into the ministry that glorify God. Whether it's a talent, gift, or something that you've worked to develop, learn the discipline of keeping your mouth shut.

Some ministers talk too much and some gossip. Don't be one of them. If you are one of these, now is the moment to change your life. Nothing good comes from repeating tales or community scuttlebutt. When you hear something negative, or maybe distasteful about someone, it should never come from the minister. The minister should never be a fountain spouting information to any who will pause and listen.

When you are gathering with other ministers or a friend there is always much to talk and laugh about, but it should never be the faults or the problems of others.

Too many times Christians gather in prayer groups. One says, "Pray for John Doe, he cheated on his taxes and owes a big penalty. He might even have to go to jail. He has become a bad person." Or another says, "Pray for Susie because she is running around on her husband and they are about to get a divorce." Or another says, "Let's pray for Rev. Joe because he isn't paying his bills and the elders and the deacons are ready to throw him out of the church parsonage." You get the gist. Often, we convey too much information about people. Most of the time, we do not have all of the information. We don't know the whole story. What we may have been told could have completely changed. How are we helping the person by telling the troubles of their lives? We only make their troubles worse. We become a part of their trouble by telling their trouble. You do not need negativity in your life. You don't need to be a part of the other person's problem.

Often our best prayer requests are unspoken prayer requests. Even when you mention someone's name, others wonder what is going on with the person.

Many times, people will request prayer for themselves saying, "I am fighting cancer. Please everyone pray for me." Another says, "I need a job. I am hurting. My family is struggling. Please pray for me." Another says, "My family is in trouble. Please pray for me." Often, people voluntarily bring others into their circle of troubles and fears by telling the nature of their troubles, then, everyone knows. It's one thing if they do it and another if you or someone else does. If someone is requesting prayer for himself, then it's his prayer request. Whoever is requesting prayer will share what he or she is comfortable sharing.

There is a fine line between telling too much and not telling enough. If you need people to pray for you because you are fighting a terminal illness, they need to know what they are praying about. If the life situation is grave, then people need to be made aware so that fervent prayer, may be offered. If the prayer request or the life matter seems insignificant, people are apt to treat it as such. A dire circumstance requires dire prayer and plain communication about what is happening. James 5:14 says, "Is anyone among you sick? Let them call the elders of the church to pray over them and anoint them with oil in the name of the Lord." The imagery here is of fervency. There is the recognition of a human need, and divine intervention. The person submits himself. There is no holding back. There is a real issue, as well as the healing and helping power of God.

When you are hungry, financially broke, and you cannot feed your children, then you call for help. That may be embarrassing. That may not be what you ever anticipated, but you call for help. You can go to the food bank. You can go to whatever charity is available. You can go to your family. You can knock on your neighbor's door. You beg if you have to because you don't want your children to suffer or be hungry. The need is communicated and made very plain that you are without food, and you are desperate for help. That is not anything that you hint about, but you are clear and plain in your conversation.

From Luke 11: 8, we have this text, "I tell you, even though he will not get up and give you the bread because of friendship, yet because of your shameless audacity he will surely get up and give you as much as you need." Jesus told the story of the man who had family that had shown up unexpectedly and he didn't have any food. He goes to his neighbor's house and knocks on the door repeatedly begging for him to get out of bed and please give him some food for his family. Not many people would ever want to do this but Jesus pointed out the importance of clearly expressing ourselves to God in prayer. Jesus said, "Ask and it shall be given you, seek and you shall find, knock and the door shall be opened unto you," Luke 11:9.

So, when we pray, we lay it all out on the line in prayer with God. There are no secrets in your life when it comes to God anyway. He knows all about you. He knows before you even ask. He knows all the good, and all the not so good. When you pray, be honest with God. You may want to be completely honest with others when you pray, or you may not. Often, people don't need to know everything. You can simply say, I need prayer for my surgery. I need healing for my disease. I need healing for my virus. Often, the level of prayer support that you receive may be in direct response to what and how you communicate your need for prayer.

Again, it's one thing when we openly communicate our needs to God or someone else. Keep in mind, in most cases, whoever you talk to besides God will probably repeat what you said and often add their perspective. Some people have the gift of keeping a confidence or a prayer request in sacred trust. Some feel as if their mission in life is to tell the news as quickly as possible to everyone. Sadly, the news they are telling is not the "good news" Jesus told us to be telling, but they are telling everyone else's news and gossip.

I want to stress this to you today. If you, your spouse, and your family can develop the discipline of keeping your conversations, what you know, your personal lives, your problems, and your struggles in your family, you will be happier. Getting everyone else involved in your lives never brings peace or fulfillment.

That certainly does not mean you cannot have a fulfilling friendship. Friendship should never mean that everything you know, whether good or bad, has to be put out on the table in dialogue. You would hope that in a real friendship, confidences would never be repeated. Some good friends can keep a confidence, but so many cannot. Too often, they can't wait to call a mutual friend to say, "Guess what I just heard." Keep your marriage between you and your spouse. Keep your family issues within your family. Keep what you have heard about others to yourself. When someone tells you something in confidence, then you must keep it confidential. There is much in life that only you and God know together, and that's okay. You can trust God with what the two of you know, and you two can work it out.

One more word here as we remember the scripture, "Therefore confess your sins to each other and pray for each other so that you may be healed. The prayer of a righteous person is powerful and effective," James 5:16. There is a time when you or any of us say, "It's me, oh Lord standing in the need of prayer." There are those times with a friend, a Christian brother or sister that you say, "I failed. I sinned." Do you need to tell the long version of your sin, drawing it, describing it in vivid detail? Some people like to do this as it often briefly commands an audience.

I have heard preachers and Christians go into detail about their past lives because it was interesting and sometimes colorful or dynamic. However, when the congregation got up to go home, they would often go and tell how bad or colorful the person had been who had told the story. The point should always be, "Look what God has done. Look how God has changed me."

I cannot finish this chapter without including this text from James chapter 3: 3-12. He wrote the following passage about taming the tongue. "When we put bits into the mouths of horses to make them obey us, we can turn the whole animal. Or, or take ships as an example. Although they are large and driven by strong winds, they are steered by a very small rudder wherever the pilot wants to go. Likewise, the tongue is a small part of the body, but it makes great boasts. Consider what a great forest is set on fire by a small spark. The tongue also is a fire, a world of evil among the parts of the body. It corrupts the whole body, sets the whole course of one's life on fire, and is itself set on fire by hell. All kinds of animals, birds, reptiles, and sea creatures are being tamed and have been tamed by mankind, but no human being can tame the tongue. It is a restless evil, full of deadly poison. With the tongue, we praise our Lord and Father, and with it, we curse human beings, who have been made in God's likeness. Out of the same mouth come praise and cursing. My brothers and sisters, this should not be. Can both freshwater and saltwater flow from the same spring? My brothers and sisters, can a fig tree bear olives or a grapevine bear figs? Neither can a salt spring produce fresh water." James stresses the power of the tongue. He also underscores the importance of us controlling our tongues.

You will need to decide how you conduct your mouth. Put God in charge and try to let the Holy Spirit filter what comes up in the bucket and out of your mouth. We don't always do that. Let God be in control of what you say, and how you say it.

Let's end this chapter with Philippians 4:8 "Finally, brothers and sisters, whatever is true, whatever is noble, whatever is right, whatever is pure, whatever is lovely, whatever is admirable-if anything is excellent or praiseworthy-think about such things."

If this is where our minds are, then the same will come out of our mouths. In the prior verse, Paul wrote "And the peace of God, which passeth all understanding, shall keep your hearts and minds in Christ Jesus." There is nothing better than the peace of God. When your thinking is right, and your speech is right, your life will be right, and you will be at peace with yourself and God.

Chapter 18

Mental Health Issues

Mental illness has exploded on the scene over the last few years. It has always been in the world, but we are more aware and informed about it than ever before. Who can say if there is more now than what we had in the mid-1900s or early 1900s? Our world has gone through so many turbulent, wrenching times that every era has experienced traumatic periods of grief, depression, and emotional distress.

Throughout the years, generations have learned to struggle through dark periods and hurts. Often, people and families had no other choice but to band together and try to cope. Sometimes people could not cope, nor could their families, and they ended up being placed in facilities where no one would want to be. The critically, mentally ill were confined to mental hospitals, insane asylums, or prisons. No one wants to end up there. You do not want anybody you care about to spend their life in such a place.

Today, mental illness is talked about openly. We hear about actors and athletes coming out and talking publicly about the mental issues they have experienced. Medication for depression, anxiety, attention deficit is advertised. Millions of dollars of these medications are sold annually around the world. There is no longer a stigma associated with taking an anti-depressant because so many people do. It is no longer swept under the rug that someone sees a mental health counselor or psychiatrist. Licensed Clinical Social Workers have grown in numbers over the years. These careers, along with psychologists, Christian/ Biblical counselors, life coaches, addiction counseling specialists, chaplains of every sort, and pastors who major in pastoral care, have all exploded. Sadly, there still are not enough of these people to address the growing need because the mental illness on the planet is so great.

There are also divisions of mental illness as well as extremes. There is the person who is total mentally disturbed, needs stringent medication regimens, therapy, intense medical psychiatry, and maybe even incarceration to keep them from injuring themselves or others. The pendulum then swings to the other spectrum where everyday people deal with the blahs, feeling down, disappointed about life, anxious, scared, nervous, and filled with uncertainty. These feelings can be bad, and if we are not careful, they can be blown out of proportion. For this reason, we have different levels of counseling and various types of professionals to help people on all different levels.

Most people do not need to spend hundreds or thousands of dollars on a medically trained psychiatrist who might load them up on medication to get them through life. Some do, but not most. The majority of people just need to figure out a way. They are looking for a direction, a path, a solution to their problem, or problems. Often this is somebody to talk to. Someone who will listen, and someone who has enough background, education, and life experience to offer real suggestions and help.

Sometimes people just need someone to listen and pray with them. Often, people need more than a prayer. They need to be heard, and they need some real counseling. Pastors and ministers from all walks of life will mess up when trying to take this on because they are not trained, counselors. Ministers may be trained in the scriptures. They may be trained in prayer and sermon preparation. That helps, but often people need some real professional help. Up to a certain point, ministers can be very helpful. Often, people just need a prayer and a scripture. Sometimes some exposition of the scripture may be exactly what someone needs to hear. Too many times, people come to ministers with deep problems that are well above the average minister's level of training. They may have lost a child. They could be going through a painful divorce. It may be a financial disaster that has them on the brink of suicide. It could be an evolving mental illness that has been developing and becoming worse.

Be smart and recognize these are scenarios that you should refer to someone else. They are over your head. Frequently, you can hurt these people by trying to help them. You would not want your general dentist doing oral surgery on you if they are untrained and unlicensed for such a procedure, would you? Of course not. Too many people mistakenly see the minister of the church as someone who can cheaply solve their problems. They are going to come to you. Take hours of your time. Expect you to make them feel better and not pay you a dime for your time. Some believe that, because they occasionally put $10 in the offering plate, this gives them carte blanche access to you, your time and, your life. They can take the life right out of you. Just beware. Beware, and again I say beware.

Churches and all ministries need someone on staff or connected to the ministry, who is trained in some area of counseling. A church or non-profit can have a Christian counselor who is trained to successfully work with lower-level issues. They also must be trained to take sufficient time to determine when someone should be referred on to someone else. Trying to push an oak tree through a peephole is impossible. Too often, this is what happens when you repeatedly see the same people with the same problems. This situation never gets better.

Church youth ministers, children's ministers, and other staff positions often deal with young people or children who have severe issues and problems that need medical attention or counseling by a trained professional. Do not let your church put you in this position of trying to counsel youth and children who may need trained help or even medication. Again, there are many cases where teens and children need a Christian friend who can mentor, encourage, provide spiritual common sense, and biblical direction. Growing up, most of us needed more of this mentoring. So many young people are clueless about what they want to do, be, or pursue with their lives. Often, they have not had a parent or mature person to work with them and help them with ideas, direction, and some everyday life coaching. That is very valuable. One of the best ministries a church, a school, or an organization can offer is guidance counseling. However, it needs to be more than one 20-minute session each school year. Guidance counseling takes time. It requires listening and providing information. Answering questions and offering a wide spectrum of available life directions as well as ideas of how to get on the right paths are valuable vocational services.

With all this said, the average minister is bombarded with crazy people. With so much mental illness in the world, plenty of it has landed in the seats of almost every church on the planet. There are not any churches that do not have a few crazy people as members. I cannot prove this, of course. I have been in enough churches, pastored enough churches, served on enough church staffs, and have heard from enough ministers who deal with difficult people to believe my statement is accurate.

I rejoice if you feel you are in a mentally whole congregation. Chances are you may not be the minister and have limited knowledge of what people in the church are dealing with emotionally. Also, I realize crazy may be a stark word to use. Again, I am not referring to someone who babbles nonstop, cries, lashes out at imaginary people, and exhibits major psychological issues. Often, it is the person who calls you every day on the phone to let you know that they feel bad. Or, it is the person who may stop by your office or house often to tell you they are depressed. Or, it may be the person who is waiting for you every time you come out of your office to extract 20 minutes of your time. Or, it may be the person who has undermined every minister who has served the church. In cases such as that, you will not be the exception. They found ways to make the previous ministers miserable, and they will certainly find a way to make you miserable as well. So, crazy may not be the correct description in all cases, but on some level, there are problems. Emotionally, they are hurting. They need attention. Things are not right in their lives. They are suffering on some level, and thus there is a form of craziness that exists. As a minister, this craziness will drive you crazy if you are not extremely cautious.

I realize that some may think my use of the word crazy, throughout this chapter, is not the best choice of words, really? What should I call the person who calls the minister three or four times a week to talk about the least little thing and normally not much of anything? What should I call the person who stalks the minister in the hallways of the church daily and wants to constantly engage in small talk? Or, what about the person who has daily questions about the Bible or life in general? What about the person who is sitting in the secretary's office almost every day of the week lying in wait for the minister to come out of his or her office so they might ask a question or share some "tidbit" of information? Are these people crazy, or are they just a pain in the neck? What about the person who insists that you come by to visit almost weekly? Are they extremely lonely, or are they testing the minister's patience? What about the people who infiltrate your church and who live to serve as your deacons, elders, leaders, committee chairpersons but make it their priority to question or oppose everything you support and are trying to accomplish?

During a church meeting, a deacon spent five minutes advocating a position on something we were discussing. I had advocated the same position, in a prior meeting. When he finished his speech, I simply affirmed what he said and further added, "That's a good idea and the direction we need to go." He immediately faced the rest of the group and said, "I want to change my position immediately." Perhaps he was not crazy, but just a jerk.

There are those you will face in the church who are legitimately off their rockers. Some are emotionally needy people. Some are very lonely. Some are simply jerks. They are mean and have no sense of decent human behavior. Whether these people are crazy or not, they can deplete your energy and leave lasting emotional wounds.

The average minister has some bite marks left by mean church members. Dog bites hurt, and bites from people hurt. As we have already discussed in this book the tongue can do damage. Often, it is more than just the tongue. It is also actions where the person is on the telephone saying whatever they can to hurt the minister. Speaking against the minister, Speaking negatively. Undermining him or her.

People will frequently utilize the word "leadership." Leadership is a generally vague word that is defined in different ways by whoever is using the word. It is often the word that people begin throwing around when they want to undercut your ministry. They will start making statements like, "He needs to demonstrate leadership. Our church needs leadership in the area of outreach. Our church needs leadership with our small groups. Our church needs leadership with our giving." You may be doing everything humanly possible to reach people through outreach, building small groups, and encouraging people to grow in giving. Yet, some people will still find ways to attack you by generically saying, "We really need leadership in the church." Frequently this is a small seed planted that will grow. Usually, the person using the word is saying, "I want more personal attention. I want to be seen more. I want to be heard more. I want to know that I have clout in my church."

Consider one of the problems Jesus faced in his day-demon possession.

In Mark chapter five, Jesus restores a demon-possessed man. "5 They went across the lake to the region of the Gerasenes. ²When Jesus got out of the boat, a man with an impure spirit came from the tombs to meet him. ³This man lived in the tombs, and no one could bind him anymore, not even with a chain. ⁴For he had often been chained hand and foot, but he tore the chains apart and broke the irons on his feet. No one was strong enough to subdue him. ⁵Night and day among the tombs and in the hills he would cry out and cut himself with stones.

⁶When he saw Jesus from a distance, he ran and fell on his knees in front of him. ⁷He shouted at the top of his voice, "What do you want with me, Jesus, Son of the Most High God? In God's name don't torture me!" ⁸For Jesus had said to him, "Come out of this man, you impure spirit!"

⁹Then Jesus asked him, "What is your name?"

"My name is Legion," he replied, "for we are many." ¹⁰And he begged Jesus again and again not to send them out of the area.

¹¹A large herd of pigs was feeding on the nearby hillside. ¹²The demons begged Jesus, "Send us among the pigs; allow us

to go into them." [13]He gave them permission, and the impure spirits came out and went into the pigs. The herd, about two thousand in number, rushed down the steep bank into the lake and were drowned.

[14]Those tending the pigs ran off and reported this in the town and countryside, and the people went out to see what had happened. [15]When they came to Jesus, they saw the man who had been possessed by the legion of demons, sitting there, dressed and in his right mind; and they were afraid. [16]Those who had seen it told the people what had happened to the demon-possessed man—and told about the pigs as well. [17]Then the people began to plead with Jesus to leave their region.

[18]As Jesus was getting into the boat, the man who had been demon-possessed begged to go with him. [19]Jesus did not let him, but said, "Go home to your own people and tell them how much the Lord has done for you, and how he has had mercy on you." [20]So the man went away and began to tell in the Decapolis how much Jesus had done for him. And all the people were amazed."

The man was in serious pain. His life was shattered. He lived among the tombs. People were terrified of him. Is this the same man who is walking the halls of some of our churches? Maybe not to this extent. Or, maybe to some degree. Too often, people have joined the church without having any real personal experience with Jesus. They are still lost. Sometimes, they can converse religiously but, inwardly there is a darkness that needs the cleansing blood of Jesus. Often they need a serious dose of medication and the skills of a mental health professional. However, never rule out that there may be those lurking in the hallways of your church whose problems are much more sinister.

From Acts chapter 16 comes this passage about Paul and Silas, "[16]Once when we were going to the place of prayer, we were met by a female slave who had a spirit by which she predicted the future. She earned a great deal of money for her owners by fortune-telling. [17]She followed Paul and the rest of us, shouting, "These men are servants of the Most High God, who are telling you the way to be saved." [18]She kept this up for many days. Finally, Paul became so annoyed that he turned around and said to the spirit, "In the name of Jesus Christ I command you to come out of her!" At that moment the spirit left her.

[19]When her owners realized that their hope of making money was gone, they seized Paul and Silas and dragged them into the marketplace to face the authorities. [20]They brought them before the magistrates and said, "These men are Jews, and are throwing our city into an uproar [21]by advocating customs unlawful for us Romans to accept or practice." The story continues that Paul and Silas were arrested, badly beaten, and imprisoned. God shook the prison that night and provided a way out for Paul and Silas, but it was a brutal experience for them.

Many ministers have suffered beatings because of their confrontations with people like these in Paul's day in Philippi. Those who are possessed with demons will often harass you like this girl was being used to harass Paul and Silas. Often, some people walk with such demon-possessed people. When you confront the demon-possessed person, his or her crowd will attack you for your stand. Thus, you must consider their internal relationship with God. If they are walking in fellowship with a demon-possessed woman or man, then they likely have no real relationship with God through Jesus. Again, like Paul and Silas, these people will find a way to hurt you. Paul and Silas survived it. God took care of them. God will take care of you too my friend. God will provide a way. God may send an earthquake, an angel, or a miracle out of the sky, but if you are God's man or God's woman, he will not let the devil or the demons possessing someone else destroy you. It may seem at the time that they are destroying you, but God will provide a way of escape.

The Bible says, in First Corinthians 10:13" There hath no temptation taken you but such as is common to man: but God is faithful, who will not suffer you to be tempted above that ye are able; but will with the temptation also make a way to escape, that ye may be able to bear it."

From Acts 12:7 we have this verse where it appeared Peter had no way of escape from a prison cell but the Bible says, "Suddenly an angel of the Lord appeared and a light shone in the cell. He struck Peter on the side and woke him up. "Quick, get up!" he said, and the chains fell off Peter's wrists." And in the next verse, we read, "Then the angel said to him, "Put on your clothes and sandals." And Peter did so. "Wrap your cloak around you and follow me," the angel told him," Acts 12:8.

From Acts 9: 23-25 "After many days had gone by, there was a conspiracy among the Jews to kill him, [24]but Saul learned of their plan. Day and night they kept a close watch on the city gates in order to kill him. [25]But his followers took him by night and lowered him in a basket through an opening in the wall."

You will not escape every attack. There will be those occasions in ministry when you feel like you have been stoned and left for dead. From Acts 14: 19-20, we read again about Paul, "Then some Jews came from Antioch and Iconium and won the crowd over. They stoned Paul and dragged him outside the city, thinking he was dead. [20]But after the disciples had gathered around him, he got up and went back into the city. The next day he and Barnabas left for Derbe." They thought Paul was dead. That means that he was seriously injured. Sadly, you will meet up with people in the ministry who will detest you, resent you, and hate you enough to hurt you. Hopefully, not enough to stone you. Possibly enough to terminate you just because they have decided that they do not like you. They can cut your pay. If you are living in a church parsonage they can have the utility companies cut your electricity or water off. Or, they may tarnish your reputation enough that no ministry or congregation will ever hire you again.

Hopefully, nothing like this will ever happen to you. You have to beware. A group of religious people was not very nice to Jesus. People who are mentally ill, demon-possessed, or religiously evil are a source of pain that you will have to face with all of God's help, God's angels, and the fullness of the Holy Spirit. I will add here, Jesus arose from the grave. They killed Jesus, but he came back to life. They stoned Paul, but he got up and had a great ministry. Remember this, "If God be for us, who can be against us," Romans 8:31. And remember, "Ye are of God, little children, and have overcome them: because greater is he that is in you, than he that is in the world," 1 John 4:4.

Here is one further reminder to us all. As Paul wraps up his letter to the Ephesian Christians, he adds this exhortation from chapter 6:10-20, "[10]Finally, be strong in the Lord and in his mighty power. [11]Put on the full armor of God, so that you can take your stand against the devil's schemes. [12]For our struggle is not against flesh and blood, but against the rulers, against the authorities, against the powers of this dark world and against the spiritual forces of evil in the heavenly realms. [13]Therefore put on the full armor of God, so that when the day of evil comes, you may be able to stand your ground, and after you have done everything, to stand. [14]Stand firm then, with the belt of truth buckled around your waist, with the breastplate of righteousness in place, [15]and with your feet fitted with the readiness that comes from the gospel of peace. [16]In addition to all this, take up the shield of faith, with which you can extinguish all the flaming arrows of the evil one. [17]Take the helmet of salvation and the sword of the Spirit, which is the word of God. [18]And pray in the Spirit on all occasions with all kinds of prayers and requests. With this in mind, be alert and always keep on praying for all the Lord's people. [19]Pray also for me, that whenever I speak, words may be given me so that I will fearlessly make known the mystery of the gospel, [20]for which I am an ambassador in chains. Pray that I may declare it fearlessly, as I should."

Throughout all that you will face in ministry, keep in mind that millions and millions of Americans and people around the world battle depression. People battle various types of depression. Depressed people come to your church. Often they are looking to the church or you, the minister to lift them up or make them feel better. Sometimes you can. Sometimes your ministry might help, but it may not, or it may not last for very long, and they come back hoping you can make them feel better again. Often, it is ongoing or cyclical. Constantly facing these people will be a test of fortitude as they are often sad, down, dejected, and feel hopeless, and they want you to wave a hand and make their problems go away.

A current statistic states that one out of every 10 Americans is taking an anti-depressant. That is a massive amount of people on medication, and many of them are in your church. There are varying stats on this that are widely available and can be looked up. It is changing all the time, but the numbers do not seem to be getting better. More and more doctors are prescribing anti-depressant medication. If someone really needs it, then by all means, it should be taken.

However, I am a believer that less medication is better. More exercise, getting outdoors in the fresh air, gardening, and physical activity often helps. Staying inside all day and staring at the television or social media is a sure path to more depression. Sometimes, major life events happen that require medication. The loss of a child. The sudden death of a baby, or a spouse. A tragic life event such as an unexpected divorce or career crisis can hurl more at people than they can mentally cope with and medication, for a time, is completely understandable.

From the National Institute of Mental Health website, comes another statistic, "Mental illnesses are common in the United States. Nearly one in five U.S. adults live with a mental illness (46.6 million in 2017). Mental illnesses include many different conditions that vary in degree of severity, ranging from mild to moderate to severe."

The following information is taken from the website of Mentalhealthfirstaid.org. Mental health and substance use challenges can take many forms. There is depression, anxiety, schizophrenia, addiction, and the list goes on. Some of these challenges are more visible, and you might recognize them immediately. Others can be harder to see when you are not looking for them. But they are still there.

These statistics provide a look at how many people face a mental health or substance use challenge, whether we see it or not:

1. In the United States, almost half of adults (46.4%) will experience a mental illness during their lifetime.

2. 5% of adults (18 or older) experience a mental illness in any one year, equivalent to 43.8 million people.

3. Of adults in the United States with any mental disorder in a one-year period, 14.4% have one disorder, 5.8% have two disorders and 6% have three or more.

4. Half of all mental disorders begin by age 14 and three-quarters by age 24.

5. In the United States, only 41% of the people who had a mental disorder in the past year received professional health care or other services.

What we cannot do as ministers, congregations, and as Christians, in general, is to deny the reality of lots of mental illness in our world, our churches, and our own families. We cannot be ashamed of it. For years the average church person or minister in America was ashamed to admit mental illness. We had to pretend that prayer and Bible reading and more church attendance made mental illness go away. That all may help, but it doesn't always. We have to acknowledge this. Ministers and their families suffer from mental illnesses. This is tough to deal with because we are supposed to have it all together.

In recent years, more studies have been done about ministers' depression and their exposure to constant demands that put them at risk for anxiety, loneliness, feelings of isolation, fear, and worry. Altogether that takes a toll on the minister's mental health. Financial struggles, expectations of the ministers' spouses, limited time to spend with children, and the lack of family recreational opportunities add to family stress. Years ago, some "religious" type church leaders started talking about how the clergy should give at least 50 to 60 hours a week of their time to their jobs. They asserted that if the average church people were giving ten hours a week in volunteer work that they were doing more than the minister who was being paid already for 40 hours or more of service. First, very few congregants are volunteering 10 to 20 hours a week. Some retired people maybe, but if they are, that is because they have the time, resources, and desire to do so. Second, ministers are normally on call 24/7. For anyone to expect that their minister must spend all their evenings at the church building or involved in some other kind of church-related activity is ludicrous and will lead to burnout, a ministry divorce, dysfunctional ministry children, and maximum stress and anxiety.

The average minister needs a minimum of one day and evening where he or she cannot be bothered by anything church-related. Two days and evenings or more are better. You need this so you can take your family camping, fishing, picnicking, and to sporting events. Grow your family in a meaningful way. The average minister lives his or her life at the church, the funeral home, the hospital, in meetings, counseling, and preparing sermons. Then one day, he or she looks back and laments, "I wish I had spent more time with my family." Thus, the minister ends up regretting his or her ministry. That need not be. The ministry can be a wonderful, marvelous, fulfilling vocation. However, the church will let you sacrifice yourself on the altar of busyness meeting all their needs, and letting your own family go to hell. The church is not worth it. Your pulpit is not worth the sacrifice of your marriage, your children, and your emotional, psychological health. Boundaries must be established to protect you and your family.

Ministers must set parameters with the church early on. Too often, ministers are so excited to get the church job and the parsonage that they sell their souls to the minister selection committee and the church. Too often, we put ourselves on the altar of sacrifice promising to be "there," "here," and "everywhere" others think we should be at any given time. That ends up being impossible. You cannot be at the church office and the hospital emergency room at the same time. You cannot be praying with the sick and writing a fine outstanding sermon at the same time. You cannot be everywhere. Do not promise that you will try because it is impossible. You can only do the best you can do. You have to be fair to your calling and your family and yourself. Plus, you have to be fair to God.

The average minister becomes so inundated with busyness that often, time with God is neglected. Remember, this all started because you were walking with God and feeling his calling. Remember what a special time it was when God was working in your heart and calling you to serve him in a greater way? You were praying and spending time with him. Don't sacrifice this time with God to be the community errand boy doing everyone's religious work for them. Too often, I have heard people say, "Preacher, God has laid John Doe on my heart. Will you please go see him?" The preacher needs to say, "If God has laid John Doe on your heart, then you need to visit him."

Dear friend, listen to me. You are at great risk for depression, anxiety, and mental health challenges. The ministry is not all love and roses. You, your spouse, and your children are at risk. While there is lots of craziness in the pews, craziness is also in America's pulpits. With ministers, I do not think there is as much mental illness in the beginning as there can be later when the challenges, finances, worries, fears, and lack of family time has set in and taken a toll. Please know this, it is perfectly acceptable for you to get help. The church leaders, deacons, and elders should not fire you for acknowledging you are having trouble. They should work with you to give you every opportunity for help and healing. Insist on this provision and understanding before you agree to go to a ministry. We have to stop pretending that ministers are unflawed human beings and never need mental health help. It is a great profession but a very depleting profession.

Ministers and congregations must be open about the mental health of the congregation, and the staff ministers. Preach about it, talk about it, have forums and educational sessions that openly discuss mental health. This is a huge national topic! Do not sweep mental health under the carpet of the church. Do not pretend that more church attendance and serving on more committees will make mental health issues better.

Be proactive and create a church life that fosters better mental health. Do not plan a church ministry that divides families and puts a strain on families. People do not need to be at the church three or four times a week for anything. Worship, yes, Bible study yes, maybe a meeting or service opportunity, yes, but after this, please encourage your people to be about their lives and families.

Encourage your people to pursue good mental health by taking time away and focusing on a healthy lifestyle that promotes mental health. Things like vacations, family time, and devoting time to personal life are all important and healthy. Your people will also encourage you likewise to be about the same things as you encourage them.

In closing, do not try to exist with craziness. It is a miserable life for any person, family, church, or minister. Trying to coexist with someone suffering from mental issues or illness is only treading water. Treading water is tiring and goes nowhere. Pretending that it doesn't exist and just hoping you'll wake up one day and life will be better is not likely. You must be actively in search of a remedy. I have seen churches and ministers tolerate the same mental health issues for years. This can be very detrimental to the church as a whole. You and your leadership must work to acknowledge these issues and develop a game plan. Individuals who are suffering need help. If you cannot help them, they need to be asked to seek help or stay home until they are willing to do so.

There is never a silver bullet remedy for life's problems, including our mental health challenges. Being open, educated, and very aware are important in leading a healthy, productive life and having a productive ministry.

Chapter 19

Minister to All People

On the heels of the last chapter, it's imperative to affirm our call to minister to all.

Today, while many need mental help, we extend the love, grace, and message of Christ to all. All need God's love, forgiveness, help, and direction in life. Jesus died for all. The ground at the cross is level, and whosoever will, may come to Christ.

"There is neither Jew nor Gentile, neither slave nor free, nor is there male and female, for you are all one in Christ Jesus." Galatians 3:28

At this stage of our world and my life, I would have thought we would be beyond any form of racism, bigotry, or mistreatment of anyone because of skin color or ethnic background. Unfortunately, it has continued to exist in ways and at different levels throughout the world. It should never have existed. There has never been a place for racism, but sadly it is real.

We must get this to a place where there is no racism of any kind. The mistreatment of anyone because of their skin color, sex, age, geographical background, socioeconomic status, mental or physical illness should never happen.

People are people. God created us all. Every human has a heart and a soul. The mistreatment of a human being is a despicably cruel act. Often it stems from ignorance and sometimes sheer hatred. Too often, this behavior is implanted by years of exposure to a culture that inbreeds this mindset.

Today's minister is more multicultural than ever before. There was a day when the minister was exposed to only one region of the country. It might be an inner-city, or it might be a small town. It could be the heart of Appalachia or a mission field in Africa. Today our ministry is broader than ever before. Regardless of how isolated your ministry is, we are connected globally. While your ministry may be to a certain group, your message is likely to go out to the world. The Internet, social media, easy videoing of your sermons and Bible studies, and more make your ministry accessible to others. A minister in the middle of nowhere is no longer a ministry in the middle of nowhere. A minister can send out videos and Bible studies and messages and songs and educational tools around the world with a fair amount of ease. Therefore, your ministry has every chance to be very broad and include thousands of people, even if you have a congregation of 30 people.

Your attitudes, mindset, feelings, theology, prejudices, and opinions are all going to be communicated, not only to your church or ministry group, but also to your community and even beyond your community.

Today, more people are not attending church, but they may click on a device such as their phone to see what you are saying.

They may watch only five minutes, but it's five minutes more than they have ever spent in your church. What you say and think can be heard by many others.

Your ministry must be inclusive of all. In your life, your messages, your work, and your ministry, you embrace all people. You love all people. You work to help all people.

The aged people should not be locked away in a warehouse to be forgotten and ignored.

The idea that they are disposable because they are beyond 65 is cold and evil. At this writing, my vibrant 99-year-old friend still greets people at church, lives alone, and plants and tends a garden. The world is a better place because of her joy, attitude, and Christ-filled life. People age, get sick and die, but we must never look at the aged as an albatross around the neck of society. Keep your ministry strong and embracing of senior adults.

Keep your ministry filled with love toward people who have unwanted pregnancies. Millions of abortions are still occurring. Don't condemn people who are pregnant and unmarried. Love them and celebrate that they have chosen to preserve a life. Help them to see and find a way to a better place. Help them to see that the best thing they can do is have the child. If not for them, then for someone else who has been praying for a child to love and to raise. There are scenarios where the age and health of the mother come into question. There are situations when the health of the unborn child is in question. My first wife and I lost multiple babies through miscarriages. One was stillborn. There were other situations where the baby had stopped growing and developing. Don't ever try to be God with people. You aren't all-knowing. You don't need to know all their business, but you do need to love them. If you have a lady in your church who has an abortion, love her and the others involved. There may be medical issues concerning the unborn baby that you do not know about. There may be issues concerning the mother's health you don't understand. It's not your job to know everything. It's your job to let God love through you, and minister to all involved, as you have the opportunity.

Most of the time women who have had abortions feel guilty, regretful, and are hurting enough. It's not your job to make them feel worse. I'm not advocating abortion on demand in any form. I'm advocating that you minister to all people regardless of the situation. If a young unmarried lady, in your church, is pregnant, then on some level, she already feels bad. If you, your family, or others make her feel worse, she is likely to seek an abortion. Once the pregnancy has occurred, it is time to move forward with saving and caring for this mother and baby. There must be a ministry of love, support, and celebrating life.

Minister to all colors and races of people. I grew up in Appalachia and was not around anyone who was not a caucasian until I went to college. Today, I have the privilege of working with thousands of Asians, Hispanics, Africans, African Americans, Canadians, Latinos, Europeans, and so on, in doing the Lord's work. I have friends with varying skin colors from varying ethnic backgrounds. My friends from various countries around the world have a multitude of shades of skin color. To God be the glory is what I say about this. I am glad. I've always thought I would love to pastor an African American church or maybe be an Associate in an African American Church.

There is no room in this world to mistreat a person of any color. People must be loved and treated equally. Jesus died on the cross for all. The ground at the foot of the cross is level. No race or group of people stands taller before God. God created and loves us all.

More than ever, churches have multicultural congregations, especially closer to the cities and suburbs. Hispanics, Latinos, Asians, and all ethnicities make up congregations. People continue to travel and locate in other countries. As ministers, we have great opportunities to learn from others as we embrace each other to do the Lord's work.

Embrace the poor and the rich. James had a lot to say about this in James chapter 2: "My brothers and sisters, believers in our glorious Lord Jesus Christ must not show favoritism. ²Suppose a man comes into your meeting wearing a gold ring and fine clothes, and a poor man in filthy old clothes also comes in. ³If you show special attention to the man wearing fine clothes and say, "Here's a good seat for you," but say to the poor man, "You stand there" or "Sit on the floor by my feet," ⁴have you not discriminated among yourselves and become judges with evil thoughts? ⁵Listen, my dear brothers and sisters: Has not God chosen those who are poor in the eyes of the world to be rich in faith and to inherit the kingdom he promised those who love him? [6]But you have dishonored the poor. Is it not the rich who are exploiting you? Are they not the ones who are dragging you into court? [7]Are they not the ones who are blaspheming the noble name of him to whom you belong? [8]If you really keep the royal law found in Scripture, "Love your neighbor as yourself," you are doing right. [9]But if you show favoritism, you sin and are convicted by the law as lawbreakers. [10]For whoever keeps the whole law and yet stumbles at just one point is guilty of breaking all of it. [11]For he who said, "You shall not commit adultery," also said, "You shall not murder." If you do not commit adultery but do commit murder, you have become a lawbreaker. [12]Speak and act as those who are going to be judged by the law that gives freedom, [13]because judgment without mercy will be shown to anyone who has not been merciful. Mercy triumphs over judgment. James 2: 2-13.

Women and men are one in Christ. Men and women are different. Is it possible to say women and men are equal? We are two very different human beings. God was very masterful in creating the opposite sex. The nature of our creation gives us the ability to procreate. To create other human beings. That is an amazing accomplishment. Every time I have witnessed the birth of a new baby, I have marveled at what God can do through two human beings. Still, there are places on the planet where women are mistreated. Even in America, there are religious entities that keep women suppressed. Women aren't allowed to speak in church, hold an office in the church, and must dress a certain way in church. If I were a woman, I would not associate with that kind of church. Hundreds of woman pastors and teachers, counselors, missionaries, and more have graduated from Newburgh Theological Seminary. They are doing an excellent job in ministry leadership roles. Women and men have sexual differences, we are emotionally different in a lot of ways, it seems, but some even argue this point. I always thought girls' basketball was funny until a little girl, younger than I, whipped me good in several one on one games. She taught me a good lesson. For the most part, women can do anything men can do, and vice versa. Men can't have babies, of course. As far as living and serving, the Bible says we are one in Christ.

The main driving theme is, do not disparage anyone. Lift others up. Speak well of people and to people and be humble and kind toward all people. Never think that you are better than anyone because you never know whose company you are in for sure. You might have a lot of education. You may have a lot of money. You might have a lot of nice things. That is all wonderful. Praise God and thank him for his blessings. You may not have much of anything, but you are working and trying. You are learning. You are working to better yourself. This is also great. You may be at the bottom of life. You may have lost everything due to some bad decisions. You may have messed your life up, but now you are trying to recreate your life and straighten out the things of your life. God will help you if you will work with him. He can help you put your life back together. I say all this to emphasize that regardless of where you are or who you are, treat others the way you want to be treated.

Jesus taught us, "So in everything, do to others what you would have them do to you, for this sums up the Law and the Prophets," Matthew 7:12. Treat others the way you want to be treated. If everyone on this planet would treat others the way they want to be treated, then most of our problems would be solved. Jesus also said, "Love the Lord your God with all your heart and with all your soul and with all your mind. [38]This is the first and greatest commandment. [39]And the second is like it: 'Love your neighbor as yourself.' [40]All the Law and the Prophets hang on these two commandments." Matthew 22: 37-40

We should never condone sin or wrong living. When people are living sinfully, wrongfully, hurting others, doing bad things, breaking the law, then we should never affirm what they are doing. Two wrongs never make a right. However, in Christ, we should always look beyond sin to love and redeem people. Jesus died for everyone. The criminal, the wounded, and those who have sinned greatly against society can be saved and redeemed. Hopefully, through the transforming power of Christ, they can have a second chance at life. Some people may have hurt you so badly that you could never give them a second chance. That is human. That is when we need to take ourselves out of it, back away, remove ourselves and let God be in control. It is not up to us to keep a human being down. Turn the person and the matter over to God and let God do what he wants to do in the life of that person. Let God fill you with peace about that person and allow God to do his work in the life of that person. Do not live a life of bitterness and turmoil. Let the peace of God rule in your life.

May God expose you to the many great people living on this planet. May you also have a great ministry to all the people you have the opportunity to serve.

Chapter 20

Your Media Ministry

The Covid-19 pandemic opened the door for a new wave of media ministry around the planet. Many churches were already using different venues of Internet methods to extend their worship and ministry. Since Covid-19, almost everyone has plugged into utilizing the Internet to broadcast their ministry and stay connected to their church families.

Years ago, people watched Billy Graham, Rex Humbard, Jerry Falwell, Robert Schuller, James Kennedy, and a host of others. Some of the larger churches had their own television ministries. First Baptist Church, Dallas, has televised for years. At one time, Walnut Street in Louisville, Kentucky, had an impressive television ministry. For many years I had a Sunday morning broadcast from First Baptist Church, Pikeville, Kentucky. We came on every Sunday morning at 9:00 on CBS affiliate WYMT from Hazard, which is the largest station in that region of the state. That broadcast went on for about seven years. Before that, at the age of 21, I had a summer television program from WOWK, which was the ABC affiliate from Huntington, West Virginia.

I still do some occasional programming and preaching through some regional stations, have had numerous programs and services on the Inspiration network, WGN from Chicago, and few other stations. In recent years, Carole and I did a broadcast every Sunday morning from Louisville, Kentucky, on the CW affiliate. We also did a Sunday night radio broadcast on XM 131 satellite radio for eight years. We were on every Sunday night at 8:00 leading into Billy Graham at 8:30.

There was a time when radio and television were the only media ministry outlets. Today, television and radio are still powerful. If you have a good time slot on a good television network, people will see your program. There is something about being on a big television screen that is more impressive than being on someone's telephone. However, more and more people are watching Internet programming on their television. So, the chance of your ministry being on television is greater all the time, and without much, if any cost.

Historically, the greatest problem with churches having a media ministry was that it wasn't feasible to be sustained by the church budget. Television time has always been expensive. For most ministries, a good time slot on a strong station has been cost-prohibitive. Today, it is doubtful if it's worth the cost. Churches of all sizes are struggling financially. A worship service broadcast on an Internet-based social media outlet will reach the majority of their crowd and many others who are curious as well. Actually, broadcasting on social media may have become one of the greatest tools for proclaiming the word of God that has ever been utilized. Onlookers, who simply want to peer into the church and see what is going on unnoticed, can come and go and watch as much of a broadcast as they desire. They may even become interested in what they are watching and become believers in Christ and connected to the ministry they are watching.

Covid-19 forced some churches into the social media age as thousands of ministries had to find a way to stay connected with their churches. Back in the day, old-time preachers were a little harsh on people who sat home to watch church on television. For quite some time, the sick, the elderly, and the homebound have turned to the television and the radio to hear a good word from God or an uplifting song. Throughout the years, Christian radio and television have done well because they gave hungry Christians a 24-hour menu of different types of music, preaching, and programming. Today, many ministries have a way of outreaching to their congregations through hand-held devices that people can watch in their recliners, at the beach, or anywhere in the world. For many people, this type of worship may become the norm.

We have increasingly grown into a very casual age. People dress more casually than ever, and it is obvious at many worship services. That is not always the case because I have preached in some churches where people still dress up very nicely for worship. Covid-19 pushed the church to another level of informality. Many people will become accustomed to worshiping on their cell phones. Lying in bed or sitting on the sofa, in their pajamas, experiencing church will become a norm for many people. For those who want to give, they will have their churches debit their credit card every month, and occasionally they will show up at the church building. For the churches with mega buildings and mega debt on those buildings, times are tough. Many churches already had more buildings than they needed. That number is greatly increasing.

Every ministry leader and congregation must strategize as to how to keep their churches together. Small groups, Sunday school classes, children's programming, care for the elderly, and homebound have all entered a different era. The idea of connectivity has taken on a new meaning. For years we have promoted the church as a place where people go to be connected to the fellowship of other believers in Christ. Now, we have to work harder to keep our church family connected through social media devices.

There will still be big church gatherings and big crowds. No one enjoys being stuck at home for weeks and months. Many people want to be in a church service or doing almost anything other than sitting at home. But in this age, we never know when another surge of contagious disease is going to come onto the scene. That could once again drive the populations back to social distancing. It could happen off and on for the rest of our lives and ministries. Having a reliable, strategic method of connecting to people through the Internet, television, radio, telephone, and whatever other available means of communication must be a top priority for you and your ministry. If not, you are going to struggle, especially when difficult social distancing times come.

Regardless of the method of communication that you utilize, keep in mind the message you are presenting through the media. It's better to be weak in the media department and strong in the content department than vice versa. The purpose of your media outreach is to proclaim the good news of Christ. Television, satellite radio, and Internet media have more content than ever before. Truthfully, I've never had a more difficult time, than the present, finding something to watch on television that interests me. When I was a child in East, Kentucky, we had one television station. We had WSAZ channel 3 out of Huntington, West Virginia. Back then, it seemed as if we always had something to watch even though we only had one channel. Today, I surf the channels in search of something I care to watch. I do find programming. Frankly, I'm amazed by the choices that are now available.

Keep in mind that as a ministry, you cannot out entertain Hollywood. A few have tried that approach. Present a good message. Present Jesus. Teach and preach the Bible. Comfort people with the message of our Lord. Help people to be made whole, to be healed, helped, and blessed. Help whoever your audience is to know that Jesus died on an old rugged cross for their sins and that he arose from the grave. Tell them that he is coming again someday. For now, he is preparing a place for all of us. Remind them that life is short and death is sure, but in Christ, we are going to that better place that Jesus has prepared for us. Let people know that God loves them, and if they come to him, he will forgive them and in no wise cast them out. If you will do this, you will have an audience, and you'll have a media ministry.

Chapter 21

Your Personal Life

First, I have to ask, "What is this?" What is a personal life? Often, the average minister wonders if a personal life exists. We all have one, but sometimes we put our personal lives aside for God. Even though we may have given our lives for the sake of Christ, we still have a personal life. We will always have one even though the years of ministry change the landscape of our personal life. No one who enters the ministry does so without making a sacrifice of life, hobbies, family, time, future, finances, and much more.

Jesus said, "For whoever wants to save their life will lose it, but whoever loses their life for me will find it," Matthew 16:25. And then from Matthew 10:39, "Whoever finds their life will lose it, and whoever loses their life for my sake will find it."

Most ministers voluntarily, and with rejoicing to some degree, have lost their lives for Jesus' sake. Most of the time, ministers feel there could be nothing better than serving Jesus and doing his work. Sometimes there are moments when the average minister has a down day and wonders, "What in the world have I done to my life?" Or, "Why have I made this crazy career or life choice?" Often, we remember more words of Jesus who said, "No one who puts a hand to the plow and looks back is fit for service in the kingdom of God," Luke 9:62. We do not want to be or feel unfit. When we look back at what we might have done or could be doing with our lives, we wonder, "are we now unfit as God's servants?" The average human's mind is filled with every thought under the sun. While you may never have had a regret or wayward thought about the ministry, you can be assured many servants of God have wondered, doubted, pondered, and regretted their callings. People are human. When the ministry and the people are celebrating our sermons or our leadership, and loving on us, it can be an emotional high. When they are throwing rocks at us, and snubbing us as they walk by us in the hallways of the church, it is not so inspiring.

That is one reason why you and your family deserve a personal life. While some people view ministers as being on call 24 hours a day, it is not humanly possible. The minister, the staff member, the chaplain, the worship leader, the church administrator is in ministry, and ministry engulfs our lives. However, every minister usually has felt a calling to be a minister. You may not have seen the light on the Damascus road like Paul but had a different kind of personal experience. Within your heart, you probably felt a pull, a tug, a still small voice that called you into service for God. When you started doing your service for God, you felt more satisfaction and joy than you had ever felt in your life. If you have had moments or glitches in your life when you were not in ministry, you were probably more miserable than ever in your life. Ministry gets in your blood. There are the highs of preaching, or singing, or leading or accomplishing something for God. The highs are why many people hang onto ministry until they die in the pulpit. The pulpit, the steeple, and the altar become their flesh, soul, and heartbeats.

There is something about being passionate and sold out for whatever you do in life. You will be more effective when you give it your all. You will be successful when whatever you do in life is all-consuming. When you are focused on something, that focus will have your energy, time, talents, and strength. When you give all to anything, whatever it is, it will do very well.

To many, the ministry is their personal lives, 24 hours a day. That will likely enhance your success in your career. That will probably keep you doing interim ministries long after you have reached retirement age. Many men and women cannot function apart from the ministry because ministry is their life.

This does not always work out well for the minister's spouse and family. Too often the spouse and the family see how consumed you are in ministry and may feel they are not as important as your calling. If you are honest about it, they might not be as important to you. You may say they are and even believe they are, but you do not live like they are as important. Our actions typically communicate more than our words. You need to think about this. Where do your spouse and children fit into your life? They must be the most important, and you have to figure out with your ministry group, church, or whoever you work for, how to make sure they remain your first priority. Remember, the priorities should always be, God, family, and then your ministry job.

You still have to show up for work and give your career your best effort. When you are on the payroll there are expectations. Some ministers may spend too much time with their families.

You cannot have a full-time ministry job and be home three or four days a week with your spouse and family. It does not work that way. My dad worked in underground coal mining for over 30 years. I was fortunate to see him on Saturdays and Sundays. He was usually tired then. As a child, I remember how much I enjoyed being with him when we had time together. There has to be a balance between your commitment to God, family, and vocation.

The single minister has an advantage that married ministers do not have. The single minister can give 60 hours a week in service easier than the married minister with children. The church is the single minister's family. When he or she comes home, they spend hours on the telephone talking to the ministry members or visiting in the homes. I am not saying a single minister should do any more than a married minister, but not having anyone waiting on you at the house alleviates some pressure.

It is not a perfect world, and I do not know of any perfect life scenarios. Every situation in life has challenges, ups, and downs. It is within the ups and downs and the potholes in the road that we navigate, that we have to figure it out, work it out, and make it work. The planet is filled with all kinds of ministers, just like you, who are trying to make it work. They have personal problems, suffer addictions, have mental issues, marriage issues, children issues, financial dilemmas, and the list goes on. With God's help, direction, and power, they are trying to do what Jesus can help us to do, and that is to be overcomers. "I have told you these things, so that in me you may have peace. In this world, you will have trouble. But take heart! I have overcome the world," John 16:33

Keep in mind that God made you, and you are you. Forget trying to make everybody like you. Forget trying to make everybody in the church admire you or appreciate your gifts and even your calling. Many in the church see you as someone to teach them and spiritually uplift them. You are there to comfort them and make them feel better when they need you. You are their shepherd. They see you as their guide, leader, helper, problem solver, and manager of your part of the ministry in the church, regardless of your ministry position. Considering all of this, you have to work through your personal life issues and determine the course of your personal life. If being you causes people not to like you, then whose problem is that? Is it your problem? There will be some people who will like you for being you, and those people will truly be more enjoyable to be around.

All of us are originals. God made you a special person, but who did you become? We hear how Jesus makes us new. The Christian life is all about a new direction in life. It is about making a turn and being a new creature in Christ. 2 Corinthians 5:17 is so beautiful, "Therefore if any man be in Christ, he is a new creature: old things are passed away; behold, all things are become new." It doesn't get any better than this. To know that you are lost and then, to know that you are saved, and old things are passed away, and all things become new is music to the ears and hearts of any saved person in Jesus Christ. But who are you? When you became a Christian and joined the church, did you start a progression of becoming like the people in the Baptist church? Or, did you start acting like the Methodists, the Pentecostals, the Lutherans, or the Catholics or wherever you assemble? We all heard a lot about change when we were saved, baptized, and started growing up in the church. Too often, our change involved becoming like other people and not more like Jesus. Sadly, if you became like some of the people in your church, you probably did not become very much like Jesus. There are saints of God, in every church, who act like Jesus. However, there are too many, in the church, who just act the way that other people act. Showing up at church, focused on Christ, clean, well put together, in control of your life and actions, caring for your loved ones, and earning an honest living is a sweet life. So many people do not have this kind of life. When Jesus helps us to make a switch from a life of sin and misery to a life that is saved, peaceful and filled with joy, it is sweet.

Within this context of being saved, a new creation, and having a life that is complete in Christ, you still need to be you and who God made. I will never forget an old guy who used to say, "Don't be somebody else. Be yourself." When I heard him say that, I wondered if he was directing that statement to me. I had observed so many ministers as a young adult, and some I greatly admired. No doubt, I often found myself gravitating to their style of ministry, preaching style, educational attainments, and their ministerial ways. Most likely, they too had adopted practices and habits from others whom they had observed. That was not necessarily bad because when we are learning and growing, we learn from teachers, mentors, and others. I learned how to lead people to Jesus because of the time I spent with soul-winning pastors. I learned preaching skills from all of the preachers I observed and heard. Whoever you were in school will be modified as you become better informed and trained.

Forget about becoming like somebody else. Focus on Jesus and let him lead you to be who you are supposed to be.

Jesus said, "And you shall know the truth and the truth will set you free," John 8:32.

You can do a lot as a minister. In many cases, people are more accepting of ministers being real people today. You cannot be crazy acting or ridiculous. You will have to figure out what that means for you and your ministry. There are limitations to any profession. There are always expectations. You simply have to determine if "their" expectations and "your" expectations mesh. You need to put your cards on the table at the beginning of your relationship. Many ministers and ministry search/employment teams start on the wrong foot. They start out like they are dating. Everyone is pretending and being really nice and selling their pluses and positives. Time needs to be taken to understand each other and to determine if you and they or they and you are a good fit for a harmonious, ministry effort. While you truly may be desperate for a job or a ministry place of service, you do not need to move yourself and family into what will become bad for you if your goals, ministry, or lifestyle are completely different from what the church or employer wants. What happens is that too often, the average minister is so desperate for a pulpit, a youth minister's job, a worship leader's job, or a place on the church staff that they become whatever they think their employer wants them to be. After the honeymoon phase and the newness of the new job wears off, life and ministry become a drag because you are trying to theologically, or in some other way, be who these people want you to be.

Often, ministers decide they will try to convince the church or group of their point of view. That usually ends up in frustration, upheaval, and misery for everyone. Sometimes, ministers pull it off, but it has to be slow, very cautious, and with seeds of education planted along the way. Remember, seeds take time to root and grow.

As an old friend said to me, a long time ago, "Just be yourself. Be who you are. Be who God wants you to be. Do not try to be somebody else."

Whatever hobbies, entertainment, recreation, or kinds of outings you enjoy, be upfront about these in the beginning. When you are open about what you like doing, it is less likely to be used against you later. Again, "The truth will set you free," John 8:32. You may have an interest or a hobby that is fine between you and God. It does not diminish your relationship with him or your family. If your church members do not know about it, then they point a finger and say that your interest or activity diminishes your ministry or detracts from your ministry job. When you serve a church in any capacity, everybody has an opinion about anything you do. However, when you are upfront from the beginning, then you can say, "I addressed that early on. You already know this."

One more verse is from Numbers 32:23 where Moses warned the people of God, "But if you fail to do this, you will be sinning against the LORD; and you may be sure that your sin will find you out." It is always better for us to deal with what we have going on for our betterment than for others to deal with our sin to our ruin and destruction. Do not let others be in the position of being able to hurt you. When they feel like you have hidden something, even if it may be altogether legal, honest and moral, they may still use it to question your integrity, how you spend your time, or if you are doing something that takes away from what they "think" you should be doing. When you are upfront about it in the beginning, then they knew upfront, and they will have to look for something else to criticize.

Of course, never improving you, never bettering you, never educating you, is a terrible idea as well. There is a diamond in you. You probably need some polishing. The person who thinks they do not need more education, study, training, and maturity is wrong. Life is growing, developing, and becoming a better you. Becoming a better you might involve giving up some things. It might involve giving up some of your interests. Maybe or maybe not. That is between you, God, and your family.

Do not be like so many ministers who take one semester of college and then pretend to be theologians. Do not go around pretending that you are a Superman when you aren't. Once, I heard an old-time preacher say, "Our job is to please God. If we displease God it does not matter who we please." Be tight with God. If in your heart you know that you and God are right, then that is what matters. Be tight with your spouse. Be tight with your family. Then, be tight with your ministry. Too often, ministers and people in general start thinking the church or the ministry is the relationship with God. Being right with a congregation, and their expectations may not necessarily be right and tight with God. It may earn you a paycheck for a while, but churches and ministries can become very religious with lots of "acts," "rituals," "meetings," "symbolisms," and often the busywork that goes through the pretenses of Christian service. Keep an eye out for all of this and work hard to avoid traps that snare you into religious activity that end up diminishing your relationship with God, hurt your marriage, and take you away from your children.

I served one church where several of the men were happier being at the church visiting or doing anything rather than being home with their families. A church like this works the ministers to death to create more weekday activities so that the unhappy people have a place to escape.

Here is what Paul said in 1 Corinthians 9:27 "No, I strike a blow to my body and make it my slave so that after I have preached to others, I myself will not be disqualified for the prize."

Here is what Paul said in Philippians 3:12-14, "Not that I have already obtained all this, or have already arrived at my goal, but

I press on to take hold of that for which Christ Jesus took hold of me. [13]Brothers and sisters, I do not consider myself yet to have taken hold of it. But one thing I do: Forgetting what is behind and straining toward what is ahead, [14]I press on toward the goal to win the prize for which God has called me heavenward in Christ Jesus."

And then from Hebrews 12: 1-3 we read, "Therefore, since we are surrounded by such a great cloud of witnesses, let us throw off everything that hinders and the sin that so easily entangles. And let us run with perseverance the race marked out for us, [2]fixing our eyes on Jesus, the pioneer and perfecter of faith. For the joy set before him he endured the cross, scorning its shame, and sat down at the right hand of the throne of God. [3]Consider him who endured such opposition from sinners, so that you will not grow weary and lose heart."

Would I hold onto anything that would interfere with opportunities to preach for Jesus? No, I would not. Too many times, I have laid it down, given it up, or walked away because, to me, Jesus is altogether more lovely than anything I know. By God's grace, he has always provided a path or a way for me to serve him. For this, I am most grateful of all.

The Bible says, "The next day John saw Jesus coming toward him and said, "Look, the Lamb of God, who takes away the sin of the world!" John 1:29 Our main focus must always be Jesus, who has taken away our sins and given us our real purpose for living. He is altogether lovely. He is worthy of our highest commitment, love, and our best service for him.

Chapter 22

Addictions

How could such a theme ever make its way into this kind of book? Because on some level, every human being deals with different kinds of addictions, even ministers. We never see them as addictions until they have taken a negative, and sometimes life devastating toll on us, and the people who we love.

Addictions can hurt you, sometimes destroy your ministry, and even lead to your death. Financially, they can dig a hole that becomes so deep that it is hard to escape. An addiction diminishes your life, ministry, and leads to regret.

Spending money you do not have, to keep up with others, can become a serious problem. The old saying is we sometimes spend money we don't have to keep up with those people we don't like. Most ministers will make less money than a third of their congregation. The leadership of the church will rarely let you make more money than they do. In a lot of churches, this may be tough financially because your leadership may not make much money. If they don't have much money, then you aren't going to be paid a lot. I suppose one of the pluses of this is you will feel less pressure to try to keep up with others in terms of clothing, cars, jewelry, and vacation trips. Sadly, in too many cases, I have seen ministry families try to live like kings and queens in a ministry world. It doesn't mesh well. If your people are wearing ordinary everyday clothes, driving modest cars, and living in modest homes, you need to be prepared to bite the bullet and adopt the same lifestyle. If you can't do that, then don't go there, or get out of that setting. It's unfair to them and not a happy place for you to be.

Too often, I've seen ministers driving the best car in the church parking lot. They wear the most expensive jewelry and dress better than anyone in the church. I know how we can rationalize this. We say Jesus deserves the best, and we want to have and do and be the best for him. I'm not sure Jesus is really in the middle of all this. Jesus once said he didn't even have a place to lay his head. I certainly am not advocating this for you. I am advocating that you use some common sense. Invest in some nice clothes but don't overdo it. You don't need 20 tailor-made outfits. Let your congregation see that you wear the same type of clothes they do. Invest in a good comfortable car, but you don't have to have the most expensive car in the church parking lot. Let a few of the elders and deacons outdo you on having a fancier car. It will make them feel good that you are so humble and servant-minded. Don't be living in the finest house in the city. What's the point? Invest in a house that gains in value and that you or your family one day can sell for a good profit. Invest in what you need in a house. You don't need a palace in order to shine for Jesus or to live a comfortable life.

Too many people become addicted to material things. They spend money they don't have. They max out credit cards on clothes, jewelry, trips, and household items. They finance cars that have payments they cannot afford. For what reason? How does this make anybody happy? How can the stress of paying for so much add happiness to any life? So often, I've seen people who are driving the most expensive car, living in the biggest house, and wearing the biggest diamond but never smiling and looking like advertisements for vinegar. There is no fun or happiness when you have a financial noose around your neck. When you are choking, it's hard to muster up a laugh or a smile. I've known people who have filled their closets with clothing they have never worn. The tags were still on the clothes. Boxes of shoes sat on the closet racks that had never been worn. Why? What is the purpose? Is this solely to fulfill the lust of want and more? Or, is it an addiction? It's become a pattern of life. You feel better when you make that purchase, but you feel worse when the credit card bill comes in the mail. That is like the person who has become addicted to alcohol. They think they have to consume two or three drinks but then feel horrible after arguing with their spouse or doing something they later regret.

For some ministers, food becomes an addiction. I know the saying is that it's better to meet a fat man on the highway than a drunk man. Neither lifestyle is becoming for anyone, including the minister. Food is the sin of choice for too many Christians. We all need food. You can live without most things, but we can't live without food and water. We need food. We need moderate portions. Seldom does anyone need three big meals a day unless you are working physically hard. It's so easy to get into a rut with our eating. Churches are notorious for having unhealthy get-togethers. We load up on cake and pie at these meals. Donuts are often the Sunday morning sin of choice at the small group Bible study gatherings. Make it a goal to take care of your health. Portion control is a testimony of some discipline in your life. Bring your body and appetite under subjection. I've been there. I know what it's like to think I had to have a donut, a cookie, or some kind of dessert every day.

One October, I was diagnosed with thyroid cancer, and it was surgically removed. Then a few months later, I was diagnosed with prostate cancer and had radiation seed implants. My urologist told me to get off sugar, and I have. I feel better. I don't miss it. I feel bad whenever I do eat anything that contains sugar. I've lost weight and feel healthier. Eating all the time and eating the wrong things leads to obesity, bad health, and misery. Gaining control of your eating, and limiting how much food you put in your mouth makes you feel better, leads to a healthier body weight, and gives you more energy to be productive for Jesus.

Millions of Americans battle opioid addiction. Some of the more familiar names are opium, heroin, codeine, oxycodone, hydrocodone, tramadol, morphine, hydromorphone, fentanyl, and carfentanil. People die every day from abusing these drugs. Pharmaceutical companies, doctors, and pharmacies have become rich peddling these narcotics to addicts. Addicts develop lifestyles that consist of daily intake, sedation, and unproductive lives. They become committed to one thing in life, and that is making sure they can get their next bottle or bottles of pain medication. That means they are always in search of the next doctor who doesn't care whether people are healthy but are very willing to write the prescription. Often, doctors give in to the exaggerated complaints of a patient who lies about pain and other conditions to obtain their medication of choice. People consume hundreds of millions of opioids on this planet. The United States has a major health crisis with opioids. This problem is not limited to the down and out drug addict who is sleeping on a park bench every night. This is often a problem found in suburbs and church pews. It can become an issue for anyone, including ministers. Don't let such an addiction destroy you. Get help. Do whatever it takes to rid your body of dependency on a pill or drug that could even lead to your death.

I am supportive of medication when necessary. Medication should be medically necessary for better health. Some people need antidepressants. Living forever on an antidepressant will not be an abundant life for you. It may help you get through a difficult crisis. Some people may need it for a few months or even a year or so to get through the death of a loved one or another traumatic life event or illness. Hopefully, you and a good doctor will work toward your recovery and unplugging you from an antidepressant or opioid so that you can function cleanly and clearly with good health. Some people who suffer from clinical depression may require a much more lengthy treatment period or even a lifetime of treatment.

Pornography is a horrible addiction that has infiltrated the planet and even churches and pulpits. So many stories are told by Christians and ministers alike who have fallen prey to pornography. There was a time that porn was hidden undercover behind the counters of convenience stores. Today it's as accessible as a click on your computer or cell phone. A clean mind is a place of wholeness and life. A polluted mind becomes a fertile place for bad thoughts, bad ideas, and imaginations that lead to sinful and immoral acts.

Sow a thought. Reap an act. Sow an act. Reap a character. Sow a character, reap a destiny. Mentally, the Christian needs time every day to read God's word, study, pray, and reflect to be productive. The minister who is writing sermons every week and doing devotionals for his church family must have a couple of hours or more a day to study, reflect, write, sermonize, and prepare. Study time should be a productive high of reading about God and spiritual enrichment. Like any other addict, the porn addict gets locked into a lifestyle of searching for the next graphic picture, movie, or sexual scene. For a moment, it may seem and feel like an escape. Like any addiction, porn has downsides of depression, darkness, and pain. There is no way that your heart and mind are right with God if you have been using your time to fill your head with pornographic images. If you have fallen for this, it must stop. If necessary, get help. Cleanse your mind with God's word. Pornography will only hurt you, your relationship with your spouse, and destroy your family and your ministry. Like being addicted to alcohol or opioids there is not a good life or ending for you if you watch pornography.

"There is a way which seemeth right unto a man, but the end thereof are the ways of death," Proverbs 14:12

Here is what the Bible says, "⁸Finally, brothers, and sisters, whatever is true, whatever is noble, whatever is right, whatever is pure, whatever is lovely, whatever is admirable—if anything is excellent or praiseworthy—think about such things," Philippians 4:8

Gambling is a serious problem around the world. Throughout America, gambling opportunities continue to grow rampantly. Nationwide, casinos exist almost everywhere. State lotteries are everywhere. Gambling can now be done on your computer or cell phone. We have a mega casino in the town where I live. Busloads of senior adults come and go every day. Most senior adults live on fixed incomes. Many live on Social Security incomes. How can they justify throwing their money away on a slot machine or a game of chance? Money is not easy to come by. You can buy food, shelter, and life's necessities with money. Why throw it away when it can be put to good use or even used to help someone less fortunate? Sadly, people become addicted to gambling. Gambling is like anything else. It can begin with the innocent purchase of a lottery ticket that becomes a daily activity that leads to eventual days at the local casino and coming home broke. Again, sow a thought, reap an act, sow an act, reap a lifestyle.

I know a lady who second mortgaged her house because of her gambling addiction. I know of another man who lost his house and wife because of his casino gambling addiction. I know of another man who spent all of his family's money gambling and died in poverty. He left his wife with nothing except a hard life of working whatever kind of job she could find to work, after his death. Church pews and pulpits alike are filled with people dabbling in occasional gambling. Like any drug or any other vice, it can take root, grow, engulf your life, and lead only to despair, loss, and poverty.

Alcohol takes root in people's lives. What starts as a glass of wine two or three times a week becomes a glass every day, and then two to three glasses a day. You end up in your big chair, or the sofa, sedated and asleep, and your evening becomes very unproductive. You don't feel like exercising or mowing the grass or finishing your housework. Alcohol can lead to impaired driving and hurting someone else. So many people have had their lives taken from them by drunk drivers. Too many marriages could have resolved an issue or avoided a boisterous argument if alcohol had not been in the mix. Be careful. Of course, a beer at the ballgame or a glass of wine one night for dinner may not hurt you, but could it negatively impact someone else? Whatever choice you make should always be between you and God. Always protect your life and heath, the safety of your family, and the perseverance and testimony of your ministry. Be smart, be wise, and always err on the side of caution about all of this.

There are all kinds of addictions from money, to drugs, alcohol, smoking, porn, gambling, and more. These are destructive addictions. Other addictions may not be so bad, but anything that takes over your life that you can't control is a problem.

Exercise is healthy, but you can overdo it. Do you really need to run a marathon every month? You might if you're addicted to running. Do you really need to buy or start another business? You might if you are addicted to work and making money. Do you really need to be in church three or four times a week? You might if you get addicted to religion. If you are the minister and this is your job, then, of course, you are going to be at the church a lot. Too often, I see people who have too many roles in the church. They are there so much that their families are neglected. You see, even a good thing can become negative and detrimental if we don't have balance and some moderation in our lives.

Do you need to pray three or four hours a day? God is not deaf. You don't have to spend hours a day convincing him to love you, help you, or to save you. God loves his time with us. We should all meet God in prayer every day. God wants to see us do something with our lives. Pray and then be useful to him and be productive in the world where he has placed you to be.

Be alert to anything that diminishes you as a person. Jesus told these parables as read in Matthew 13: 31-33, "He told them another parable: "The kingdom of heaven is like a mustard seed, which a man took and planted in his field. [32]Though it is the smallest of all seeds, yet when it grows, it is the largest of garden plants and becomes a tree, so that the birds come and perch in its branches." [33]He told them still another parable: "The kingdom of heaven is like yeast that a woman took and mixed into about sixty pounds of flour until it worked all through the dough."

Jesus taught us what a small seed can do or a small amount of yeast. The power of a seed of faith. A seed of hope. A seed of the gospel. The planted seed of prayer. A small amount of the love and the power of God can and will infiltrate you, save you, and put you on the path of peace, and abundance of life. Beware of what the wrong seeds can do when planted. They too can take root and grow to completely engulf, and decimate your life. God is good. God is love. God is more powerful than any life-wrecking addiction, vice, or lifestyle.

Each day, take a moment to do a heart check. Monitor your life, your thoughts, and your acts. Hopefully, you take care of your car and keep it in good running order. Don't take better care of your car than you do your life. Cars need service, and so do people. Do daily service on yourself. The time you spend keeping your mind and life in order and free from anything that is leading to your demise will pay off tremendously for you, your family, and your ministry. If you don't, you can end up in a place of ruination, despair, sickness, poverty, and death. You don't want to go there, be there, live there, or even take a step in that direction. If you are struggling with something, get help now. If you have to drive 500 miles to a city to talk to someone or check yourself into someplace, then do it for your life, your family, your future, and your ministry.

Chapter 23

Your Car

Since I mentioned cars in a previous chapter, let's talk briefly about your vehicle of choice. The minister should avoid driving the nicest car found in the church parking lot on Sunday morning. That goes against the mentality of some. Some people believe that ministers are entitled to live in the nicest house, drive the fanciest car, and wear the biggest diamond. If this is a lifestyle you want to justify, that is up to you. Keep in mind the verse where Jesus said, "Foxes have dens and birds have nests, but the Son of Man has no place to lay his head," Matthew 8:20. I am not advocating poverty for you. I am advocating for you to use common sense when serving a church and making a car purchase.

I have never driven the best car found in the church parking lot. Most of my cars have been middle of the road cars. For the most part, I've had nice cars to drive and several used cars along the way. I have had transportation, and that is always the main goal with an automobile.

I served a couple of churches that had some affluent members. Several of them drove the nicest cars on the market. Some owned airplanes and expensive boats along with their high-end autos. When I was a young minister, I bought a Nissan 300 ZX and drove it for almost two years. It was very cool. I did not think much about it because so many of our members at that church drove very nice cars and lived in nice big houses. However, in that church, we still had many low-income members who drove old cars. While I didn't receive many negative or resentful comments, I did receive a couple. As always, it only takes a few negative comments to bug you. It is like having a splinter in your finger. Sometimes it does not bother you until it begins to get infected and hurt.

That is something that you will have to decide. The minister has to have a car. Two is better because you don't want to be stuck when one is being repaired. The bottom line is to drive what you can afford. Church people will find something to criticize. It is commonsense, however to not break the bank when buying a car. A car loses value as soon as you drive it off the lot. Big car payments are a strain on most preacher's budgets.

Typically, a good used car, that is one or two years old, with low miles, is one of the best buys. The car is up to date, and it may even have some warranty left. It probably will not need any major mechanical work for a couple of years if it has had routine maintenance. A car like this will be more reasonable, meaning smaller monthly payments. Smaller monthly payments mean more money left for you to buy groceries.

One time, I leased a car. I am not excited about leasing. However, I was in a very poor stage of life and needed a new car very badly. At this stage of my life, I had two young boys and a wife in a wheelchair. I needed to feel safe on the highway with my family. I also needed a vehicle that would haul a wheelchair.

I was able to lease a new Toyota Sienna van. It was pretty nice to drive for many years. At the end of the three-year lease, I knew I would be buying the car because I had over 60,000 miles on this vehicle. However, I knew when I leased it that I would most likely buy the car. I bought it with three more years of payments to make. I have never paid on a car for six years before. Three years of lease payments, and then three more years of purchase payments. That's a lot of payments! I had no choice. That is how life was for me at that time. Today, I hear about people buying cars all the time with 72- and 84-month payment plans. No doubt, by the time you pay it off, you are probably going to need another one. You always need a car, what else can you do? Nothing. Buy and pay for the car.

It seems like all of life is spent making car payments or saving your money to buy a car. If you can pay cash for a car, then God bless you. It is painful at the moment, but then it's over and you don't have to write that big check every month. Saving every month to be able to make that kind of purchase takes discipline. Discipline is something that you must develop and grow in your ministry, or you will struggle. Discipline is important in every aspect of your life, from your eating, saving money for retirement, paying your bills, and living a good life.

We all have those days when we want to throw discipline and being practical out the window. Most of us have a lot of those days. There is always a price to pay when we determine that we will be undisciplined and stupid. Sometimes this happens when we think we must have the most expensive car or the biggest house. We are satisfied briefly, but then the years of expense can be staggering and nullifies most of the happiness we first felt at the time of purchase.

Back to my Toyota van. At 100,000 miles, the engine in the van locked up and had to be replaced. That happened about two weeks before my first wife's death. At first, the service department accused me of abusing the engine due to a lack of maintenance. There was a place in our town called Grease Monkey. They had religiously changed the oil every 3,000 miles. They were able to document every oil change. The dealership replaced the engine for free. I ended up driving that car several more years, and then my son drove it for several more years. The van ended up with close to 300,000 miles on it. Eventually, I gave it to a Veterans group because we flat wore it out. Looking back, the lease and then the purchase of the car was not the worst thing in the world. I ended up owning that car for 20 years!

Most churches set some of the minster's pay aside for a car allowance. Occasionally a church or ministry will provide a car. If possible, drive your own car. You do not want to live in a church-owned house and drive a church-owned car unless they are paying you enough to have your own car as well.

Be wise. Buy a good car. Take care of the car. My suggestion is to be somewhat humble. Make sure some of your elders or deacons are driving a car that is a little nicer than yours. They are the ones who are determining your salary. They will rarely let you make more money than they are making. If you are living bigger than they are, then they are going to determine you do not need a raise when discussing the next budget. If they see you aren't living big and still have needs, hopefully, they will be more considerate when preparing the next church budget.

Chapter 24

Your Appearance

"Therefore, I urge you, brothers and sisters, in view of God's mercy, to offer your bodies as a living sacrifice, holy and pleasing to God—this is your true and proper worship. [2]Do not conform to the pattern of this world, but be transformed by the renewing of your mind. Then you will be able to test and approve what God's will is—his good, pleasing and perfect will," Romans 12:1

Growing up, the only ongoing friction that my dad and I had was the length of my hair. That was in the late sixties/ early seventies when hair was a big deal. While I lived at home, there were constant trips to the barbershop, and I never enjoyed the haircuts that he enforced. However, I didn't have a choice because our high school had a dress code. We were a public school, and our principal managed to enforce the dress code. Boys had to have neat haircuts, wear belts and socks, and have their shirts tucked in. Girls were not allowed to wear skirts shorter than four inches above their knees. That was our high school life. It wasn't bad. At the age of 18, in the middle of the seventies, it felt as if we were under a dictatorship, and we were. However, it didn't kill us, and I don't remember any riots or bloody fights in school. Due to the dress code and how we were expected to present ourselves, we were a very nice-looking high school group.

When I started attending the First Baptist Church of Inez, Kentucky, our pastor James H. Grayson always wore a suit for Sunday morning and Sunday evening worship. Sunday night preaching was almost as organized and formal as Sunday morning. We didn't have the same crowd on Sunday night as we did on Sunday morning, but church was still a big deal. The main difference was that the choir did not sing.

During the seventies, I can't remember anyone preaching on Sunday morning who wasn't wearing a suit. Occasionally, if a college student was preaching, he might only wear a dress shirt and a tie. Sometimes we would have speakers who were outrageous dressers. Their suits, shoes, and ties were flashy and looked expensive. Usually, they had personalities to match their clothes. I'm sure the senior adults wondered if they were hearing a minister or watching a vaudeville act.

I bought into all of that at an early age. After being called to preach, I started acquiring clothes and was all about dressing as good as I could to preach. I worked in a grocery store for some time, had a couple of small churches, and managed with the help of my parents to have some dress clothes for church.

During my senior year of high school, I decided I would buy a tuxedo instead of renting one…. which, of course, was ridiculous. However, I did buy a tux and wore it to my senior prom. Several times later, I actually wore it when I preached in a couple of churches. Wow, how weird I must have looked! Looking back, I would never do that again! We do some quirky things when we are immature. At 18, I was extremely immature, green, and trying to figure it all out. However, even in my present stage of life, I cannot attest to having have arrived with all-encompassing wisdom and knowledge. I have days when I feel like the older I get, the less I know. When I was a young adult preacher, I tried to pretend that I knew a lot, but I didn't. Now that I'm an older preacher, I know for sure that I don't know much. It's okay to realize that outside our little minds, there is so much more information that we have not read, attained, or even tried to understand. That is why we have to work with the knowledge and experience that we have.

John 3:16 is all you need to know to be saved and to be God's child. So many have heard John 3:16, but they have not taken this scripture to heart. You can have knowledge and information but then not act on you either. You may know the speed limit is 60 MPH, but then you are determined to drive 70 MPH. You may know what is right but act wrongly. It's great to know and learn more and more. It's also important to put into practice what we do know. Practice the part of the Bible that you do understand. Preach the Bible that you understand. Keep learning. Keep growing. The chances are great that you know a whole lot of the Bible that you still haven't preached or taught. Teach what you know. Live what you know to be the truth. Put God's word and ways into practice.

The minister's appearance has certainly changed over the years. For most of my ministry, I wore a suit on Sunday morning. When I always preached on Sunday nights, I wore a suit or sometimes simply a dress shirt. As the culture changed, I started wanting to do as many others were doing. Eventually, I started wearing sweaters on Sunday morning and became more casual. I have to admit that it was certainly easier dressing for church. I was more comfortable, and my attire was a lot more affordable than a dress suit. I have enjoyed dressing down for preaching and feeling more relaxed in the pulpit. A relaxed minister creates an environment for a relaxed church. That is good, but maybe not so good.

Frequently, there is a double-edged sword with regard to what we do. If people become too casual, then the tendency is to also become very casual about attendance, financial support, and involvement. I do not like religion, but there is something about religion that beckons people to follow the rules, such as faithful attendance, giving, and commitment. People should not give their money based on perceived religious obligations, but out of a heart of love for God and the desire to give back to him. Attendance and service should be done out of love, a desire to attend, and a desire to worship and serve. You are teaching and preaching the love of God in Christ. Jesus is about love. We serve him because we love him. We give because we love him. We are working together to spread his word and love. You will feel better about this kind of life, ministry, and preaching. A ministry where you try to push or guilt people into faithfulness by making them feel obligated to obey all the rules seems to be missing the point of our faith. The rules are still there. The Ten Commandments and the Sermon on the Mount are still applicable. God's Holy Word is our playbook for living. Teach it, preach his word in love, live his word, and God will use you. Never beat people on the head with it, you will lose them. There will always be someone who will say, "Preacher, you really let them have it today." That's probably a clue your message wasn't so great. Most likely, that person is angry about something and was glad that you poured out criticism on everybody in your preaching. Let God take care of the "pouring it on." You preach with love and with the motive of helping, ministering, and encouraging people. People need Jesus, forgiveness, and hope. Communicate God's word to them, and the Holy Spirit will do his work.

I can't tell you how to dress for ministry. I have some ideas, of course. Go to church clean. Always shower, brush your teeth, brush your hair, and smell good when you go to church or wherever else you go. You are trying to win people. You aren't going to win people if you stink or look disheveled. You may have the best sermon in the world that day, but it could fall on deaf ears if your congregation is focused on the body odor that you are emitting. Do not overdo it with colognes and perfumes. Too much fragrance is not good either. Some deodorant, clean clothes and combed clean hair, brushed teeth, and a clean mouth are all essential. Carry some breath mints. I always pop one in my mouth after speaking and especially if I'm going to be greeting people somewhere in the church.

If you are going to preach in a casual style, please still keep it clean and neat. Don't go looking like someone who just climbed out of the gutter. You are representing the almighty, all-powerful

God. Is this what you want to convey that God can do for your audience? Do you want them to believe if they live for God, then they are going to end up looking like they climbed out of a gutter? You don't want to make this kind of impression.

While I am comfortable preaching casually and enjoy it, I am leaning back to proper dress for worship and leading ministry studies and efforts. The first part of the message that people see is how you are dressed. You can be too casual in your dress, and you can certainly overdo it. Moderation is a good rule in most cases. Why not apply it to the way that you dress?

I've seen ministers who wear a navy blue suit every Sunday. It may not even be the same navy-blue suit, but it's a rather plain navy blue suit. That is smart because it still looks good, and the message is not that you are in a style show mode for Sunday worship. That keeps it simple. You can get by with two or three suits, change out your dress shirts and ties, and you are good to go. Invest in a couple of good pairs of shoes to match and switch them out. Buy a couple of new pairs of shoes a year and keep them for preaching. You'll feel more secure if you are wearing comfortable, presentable shoes.

Suits are expensive. I understand that this is why many ministers aren't wearing them today. On a meager salary, it's tough to go out and buy a good suit. Some churches have clothing budgets for their ministers, but most do not. Ministers with small salaries are up against a wall as they try to look good and buy groceries for his or her family. If you are struggling, then go with one or two suits that will work with different shirts and ties.

You might consider a robe. A lot of ministers wear robes, and this makes it real simple. You can get by with wearing the same robe every Sunday. Keep it clean and presentable. I wear robes occasionally, and they are great. You don't have to worry that much about what you are wearing underneath. When church is over, then off with the robe, and you are good for the rest of the day. If you go casual or wear denim when you teach or preach, keep it neat, crisp, clean, and presentable.

Keep this in mind about your appearance. If a state trooper pulls you over, he or she will be wearing their uniform. They are not going to walk up to your car in Bermuda shorts and flip flops. When court is in session, the judge will come out in his or her robe. They will not come out wearing exercise sweats and running shoes. The trooper or the judge appears looking, official. You take them seriously because they look official.

I remember an airline once tried to have everybody dress casually and run up and down the aisles acting very frivolous. They soon did away with that and went back to official airline attire. They figured out that people who are flying in a small metal object at an altitude of 30,000 feet wanted to be assured that professionals were caring for them and not friends from their college fraternity or sorority.

Have you noticed that the evening news anchors on television always dress well? They don't come on the air with uncombed hair, tee shirts, and denim jeans with holes in the knees. I like this kind of casual clothing. However, television executives work hard to keep viewers and sell their stations. Presentation is vital. If it is important to the media, then surely, we need to realize that how we appear in our ministry positions is even more important.

At this stage of my ministry, when I go somewhere to speak, I wear a dress suit. That is unless the host provides specific instructions concerning how to dress. Possibly, it's an occasion where everyone will be wearing robes. That happens often because I participate in ordinations and other graduation commencement services. Or, if the service is business casual attire, I don't want to stick out like a sore thumb wearing a suit. Most of the time, a suit works for Sunday worship.

When you are participating in preaching or leading ministry in any way, you need to be and look your best. You don't have to overstate yourself, but on a scale of one to ten, why settle for a five in appearance? Comb your hair, shower, put on fresh clothes that aren't wrinkled, or look like you picked them off the floor before coming to church. I use to have a dry cleaner press my suit and shirt every weekend. I would drop it off Thursday or Friday and pick it up Saturday to wear on Sunday. Always give attention to shoes. If your shoes need polishing and buffing, then do this the night before.

Prepare your heart and mind for worship. Your appearance will only take you so far. If you have a great message and are very prepared to preach or teach, don't distract from what you have to say by not giving attention to your appearance. You don't want to lose people because of the way you look before you even start talking.

All in all, do your best for Jesus. Work, prepare, and present yourself in such a way as to win as many people as you possibly can to Christ.

Here is a verse about right thinking. When it comes to presenting ourselves in ministry, we should incorporate true, noble, right, pure, lovely, and admirable into our appearance. That does not mean, in any way, that we are aiming for a "style" show presentation. Nor does it mean we are dressing down so much that it appears we are apathetic about our appearance. Our goal is to honor our Lord the best that we can. Paul said these words to these Christians, " Finally, brothers and sisters, whatever is true, whatever is noble, whatever is right, whatever is pure, whatever is lovely, whatever is admirable—if anything is excellent or praiseworthy—think about such things," Philippians 4:8. We should try to do the same in our appearance.

Just to reiterate, do the best you can, and then do not worry. After you have showered, groomed, and put on clean clothes, then go to church and preach heaven sweet and hell hot. Preach the blood of Jesus. Preach about the risen Christ. Preach about eternity and the love of God. Tell them the old story of Jesus who came to die on the cross for our sins. Tell them about the forgiveness of God and how important they are to God. God made us individually and has a plan for each of us. This is your job, your calling, and your ministry.

When you go to teach, preach, and do ministry and are overly concerned about how you look, then you are going to be obstructed in your freedom and liberty. You have to put all this aside when you get up to teach or preach. Look in the mirror before you go to your appointed place of ministry, and then move forward and do the work God has called you to do. Your ministry is about the truth of God in word, life, action, and in your appearance. Again, Jesus said, "Then you will know the truth, and the truth will set you free." John 8:32

Chapter 25

Standing Alone

Often, when there is dissension in the ministry, the minister stands alone. Most of the time, people in the congregation will want you to choose a side and, in particular, choose their side. If you try to stay neutral and let factions in the congregation work it out, they will accuse you of being a poor leader. Time and again, I have seen Sunday school classes and other ministry groups in the church get into a big project they can't handle. They will suddenly need the pastor or one of the church staff members to bail them out. Your thought may be, "You got yourself into this mess, now get yourself out of it!" When you stand back and take this position, they'll start throwing the leadership word around. They'll say things such as, "Our pastor is not leading. We need a leader." When you do step in and try to untangle the mess they've made? They may not like your suggestions or how you suggest that they untangle the mess.

Jesus said, "Behold, I send you forth as sheep in the midst of wolves: be ye therefore wise as serpents, and harmless as doves," Matthew 10:16 Jesus always knows. That is your only hope of surviving so many of the little dilemmas that come up in church life. If you barrel in as the know it all or fix it all, somebody will applaud you while most of the crowd will back off or even walk away. "From this time many of his disciples turned back and no longer followed him," John 6:66. In this text, a massive number of people couldn't understand and accept what Jesus was saying and walked away. In the average ministry, most ministers can't survive the majority of the crowd walking away. Jesus was Jesus. You aren't Jesus. So, you have to heed what Jesus said which, in other words, is, "Don't be stupid." Don't lose your ministry over fighting for a certain color of the carpet, whether curtains should be in or out of the baptistry, or 99% of the other ridiculous issues that churches argue about. I would not fight over the music either. Take it easy. Be relaxed. Don't push and shove to have a certain style of music. If you have started the church and have some control of the situation, that is different. You can make decisions and let the chips fall where they fall. When you have moved into the neighborhood, are living in a church-owned house, and just getting started, then please don't do it. Let them know up front that you are not coming into the church to take sides on the format of the worship service, the music, a picture on the wall, or how many times a month you have a carry-in pot luck dinner. You have bigger fish to fry than all these things.

I understand that music, the worship format, and all this is important. There is nothing worse than a bad format and terrible music. Either can be a downer or an upper. When it's a downer every week, it starts getting on your nerves. I've been there,and I understand. All I'm saying is to utilize the Jesus strategy, "Serpent, Dove." Take it slow and build your support, and lead them to see it as their idea. From building a building, to changing any aspect of a ministry that you inherit, take it easy and build your support. It might take years. One church building I was involved in took seven years of planning, educating, and building enough support to make it happen. When it did happen, there were quite a number of people who were against it, which made it a challenging time. The building was built and ended up being one of the nicest ministry settings in the region.

The attitude of the elders and deacons in your church is that they have to stick together. Their thinking is that they will be "there" when you are gone. In most cases, they don't want to interrupt their fellowship or fall out with each other. They are on your side as long as you are on their side. Usually, they are not on your side when you are not on their side. The Jesus strategy is your only hope.

Sometimes in small churches, you will have ten deacons or elders or a leadership team who have worked together for 30 years. There will be someone in that body who does not like one of the other members of the body. Possibly they've argued before or resent each other. They know what the pet peeve of the other one is, and sometimes they will try to get the minister to be on their side of some issue or stance. Or, maybe, just to be their best buddy to the exclusion of the other. You have to watch for that and not be pulled into that kind of ongoing church rivalry.

Some church members will be your best friends and stand with you. Some will stand with you for a long time. In most cases, when a wave in the church turns against you, no matter how wonderful your five or ten supporters are, they will not be able to save you from the tsunami of destruction. When they came to arrest Jesus in the Garden of Gethsemane, even Peter, who with a drawn sword, cut off the ear of one of the soldiers, could not save Jesus.

There will be those who stand up and take a punch for you or even go on a verbal attack for you. In the end, they won't be able to save you if it's a large wave of opposition. I'm not writing this to oppress you. I'm writing this to save you. The Psalmist said, "Teach us O Lord to number our days and apply our hearts unto wisdom." Having common sense and not going crazy in your ministry will help you to extend it and make it more enjoyable. You can still get work and projects accomplished but employ the Jesus strategy, "Wise, gentle."

Be very attuned to the word "leadership." When your church members start saying, "Our pastor does not lead." Or, "We need a minister with leadership skills," then you have to be concerned. You have to bring them together and say, "I am being accused of not leading in this particular area of concern. Will you please let me offer a couple of ideas?" They can either hear your ideas or not. If they don't want to hear your ideas then you are in trouble. If they will listen to a couple of your suggestions or options for whatever the dilemma is, then you are probably safe for the time being. Often, there are one or two people in the church, who get a splinter in their backside about the minister, and it festers. Their goal is to somehow inflict or inject their poison into other people. The "leadership" word is a vague word that's hard to define and difficult to defend. Here is someone who will say, "The minister is not a leader." The minister may say, "Yes I am." Someone else says, "No, you are not." It's not always easy to defend yourself should this become a debate.

At my last full-time pastorate, our church grew 400%. We had over 600 additions and built a gorgeous new facility. Financially our giving was the best in the church's history. We had several staff members and paid them well. We had more ministries than ever before. We gave more money to missions than ever before. We were reaching people from all walks of life and backgrounds. We all worked hard. The ministry was going better than most churches in our area. Two of three people who opposed me plugged into the "leadership" theme. They said I was not leading the church. The truth was we had come from zero to 100 and were doing great. The real truth was these two or three people had been against building our new sanctuary because it was not their idea, and they weren't on the committee that designed the project. Nor did they feel like they were prominent enough in the church and craved more and more attention and control of the church. They were very sad people who had made some sad mistakes in their lives and somehow felt a need to find satisfaction by being prominent at the church. I was at the church for ten years, had a great ministry, and was able to move on to greater ministries. However, I know the sting of the vague leadership word. You can only do your best. Your response is, "Here is where we are, and here is what we can do." Or, "Here is where we have been, and this is where we are." Or, "Here is how we can try to remedy our dilemma."

Sometimes no matter what you say, people will put their hands over their ears and act like crazy people. They don't want to hear your thoughts. They don't want to be led. In reality, they don't want leadership. Remember the story of Stephen? "On hearing this, the members of the Sanhedrin were enraged, and they gnashed their teeth at him. [55]But Stephen, full of the Holy Spirit, looked intently into heaven and saw the glory of God and Jesus standing at the right hand of God. [56]"Look," he said, "I see heaven open and the Son of Man standing at the right hand of God."

[57]At this they covered their ears, cried out in a loud voice, and rushed together at him. [58]They dragged him out of the city and began to stone him. Meanwhile, the witnesses laid their garments at the feet of a young man named Saul.

[59]While they were stoning him, Stephen appealed, "Lord Jesus, receive my spirit." [60]Falling on his knees, he cried out in a loud voice, "Lord, do not hold this sin against them." And when he had said this, he fell asleep," Acts 7: 54-60.

Of course, not too many of us want to be drug out of the town and stoned. To some extent, ministers have been pushed out of town and left for dead. In too many cases, the leaders of the church hope they have maimed you enough so that you never minister again. In some cases, they will do all they can to prevent you from having another ministry. Too often, they will get involved in the place where you are trying to move to and try to circumvent you from moving on to another ministry. That is a form of evil that I don't understand. There comes a time when the minister and church relationship ends. When the time comes, the minister and church should agree that it's over, and everybody should move forward in their different directions. The minister should leave the church alone, and the church should leave the minister alone. The church should not try to interfere in the minister's next ministry setting or his or her next job. It's no longer their business. If the church, in any way, tries to interfere with your next ministry job or any job, then you need to scrape together whatever money you can to hire an attorney to defend you. You might have to go into debt and have the attorney develop a payment plan for you. It would be better for you to do this than to let any group harass you after you have determined to leave and go to another place of service.

I certainly hope this never happens to you. If I don't warn you, no one else will. I'm not necessarily writing this book to make friends. I hope you'll be my friend because I'm like you and I want people to like me. However, I'm writing this to try to help you avoid the pitfalls of ministry. Again, pay attention to what Jesus said, "Be wise, be a dove." Also, when the time comes, it's about saving you and your family. Don't be afraid to throw rocks back at them if it becomes necessary.

Many years ago, a congregation gathered to fire a friend of mine. He had served there for 20 years. An attorney friend of his from another state happened to come to the church that day. It was a coincidence but probably a God-incidence. As the service started, my friend stood up and welcomed his attorney friend from Texas to the church and introduced him by saying, "This is Attorney John Doe, and he takes care of my business in Texas, and he is with us today." Not a word was brought up about terminating my friend that day. Everything got quiet, and my friend stayed another ten years at the church.

Sometimes it doesn't take much to quell the storm. Sometimes, you are frantically rowing the boat and holding on for dear life. Hold on. Hold tight. Keep your family together at all costs. Do what's best for your family and you. Do whatever is necessary. Be gentle, be wise, utilize counsel, demonstrate as much leadership, concern, empathy, and team effort as humanly possible. Make changes if you can and need to do so. No minister is perfect. Sometimes the congregation may have a valid point, and you may need to step it up, change your attitude, or do your ministry differently. If you are married, pray about this and talk with your spouse. Sometimes you can talk to a trusted friend from another town but be wise about seeking counsel.

Ministers aren't perfect, and we aren't always right. Do everything you and God together know to do. Build your rock pile, if necessary, hire an attorney when nothing else seems to be working. Whatever you do, do not sit back and do nothing.

When all is said and done, God has called you. You belong to him. Nothing is impossible with God. God has something better for you. There always comes a time to put the past behind you. If you hold to the past you will surely dry up, wither and die. Take hold of God and his power and go forward.

Life and ministry are today and hopefully tomorrow.

Chapter 26

Do Your Best

The minister who never shows up will not be in the ministry very long. If you can get by with not showing up for a while, it will be a short while.

A few ministers and very, very few, have set themselves up in ivory towers and committed themselves to only study and preach. Study, quiet time, and preparation are the minister's priorities if you are going to deliver God's word. But if you never show up when people need you, eventually, they won't want to hear what you are saying.

Going to the hospital, funeral home, graveside, nursing home, and taking emergency calls are all part of the ministry. People don't want a card from you two or three weeks later. They want to see you and hear from you. They want a word from God. They need God during these tough times. The minister must break away from whatever he or she is doing to go and stand with the ones who are suffering.

If you have a big church, then you may have several ministry staff members who have different roles. When you have thousands or hundreds, it is difficult to be everywhere. That is why some ministers get tired. There is a difference between being tired in the work and tired of the work. Doing the work of ministry may make you tired, but you will be energized as you fulfill your call and do the work God has called you to do.

Ministry is tiring and draining when we have to battle the parts of church work, we never felt called to do like, refereeing church division and squabbles. That is what tires you out. You don't get tired of praying with people in the hospital, or the funeral home, or trying to help someone through grieving the death of a family member. You don't get tired of reading the Bible and preparing a message or a song to sing or planning for teaching or a ministry event. No. That is what you have been called to do. That is what you love to do. We don't get tired of doing what we love to do and are called to do. Physically yes. Mentally, only if we have so many visits to make, they might be hard to fulfill in one day. That can be trying. Usually, it's stimulating that you are needed, wanted, and you are delivering something that a doctor, an attorney, an engineer, or no one else can deliver. You are delivering Jesus. You are going into a home or an emergency room to try to help deliver the peace that passes all understanding.

You must have a day off. Your family must take a vacation. You must spend lots of playtime with your spouse and children. If you do not, you will look back and have regrets. However, you have been called to a ministry. You have given yourself to ministry. You are God's special agent of communication and help. You are the Lord's arms, feet, and voice. So, show up when people need you. When you hear someone has been hurt and taken to the emergency room, go to have prayer. Most people will welcome prayer in any time of crisis. When you have not been invited to preach the funeral of a deceased church member or someone connected to your church family, go to the funeral home anyway. When someone is suffering and needs prayer, do your best to find a moment to pray with that person.

After two or three hours of reading, study, prayer, and preparation, I have always been ready to get out of any building. Some ministers can sit in their church buildings all day. I've never really enjoyed sitting in an office. Some church leadership makes it difficult because they will say, "Why isn't our minister out visiting the sick?" When you are out visiting the sick, they will say, "I stopped by the church to see the minister, but he is never in his office. I can never find the minister at the church." That is something that will frustrate you. If you try to be everywhere, you think everybody wants you to be, then you will never be where you are supposed to be. Be where God wants you to be, and you will be okay. You and God can figure this one out. If people need to see you at your church office, then mutually agree on an appointment time. That saves everyone frustration.

Paul said, 9 Let us not become weary in doing good, for at the proper time we will reap a harvest if we do not give up," Galatians 6:9

"Do your best to present yourself to God as one approved, a worker who does not need to be ashamed and who correctly handles the word of truth," 2 Timothy 2:15

"Do you not know that in a race all the runners run, but only one gets the prize? Run in such a way as to get the prize. [25] Everyone who competes in the games goes into strict training. They do it to get a crown that will not last, but we do it to get a crown that will last forever." 1 Corinthians 9: 24-25

"Commit to the Lord whatever you do, and he will establish your plans," Proverbs 16:3

"Whatever you do, work at it with all your heart, as working for the Lord, not for human masters, [24] since you know that you will receive an inheritance from the Lord as a reward. It is the Lord Christ you are serving," Colossians 3: 23-24

"Therefore, since we are surrounded by such a great cloud of witnesses, let us throw off everything that hinders and the sin that so easily entangles. And let us run with perseverance the race marked out for us, [2]fixing our eyes on Jesus, the pioneer and perfecter of faith. For the joy set before him he endured the cross, scorning its shame, and sat down at the right hand of the throne of God. [3]Consider him who endured such opposition from sinners, so that you will not grow weary and lose heart." Hebrews 12: 1-3

You and God always know when you are trying to do your best for him. Love God, love, and take care of your marriage and your family. Daily, live, and do your best for God in your mind and heart. Do your best in the ministry that you are called to do. At certain times, people will tell you that you are doing a good job. Thay is usually when you have been there to help them in some way. A favorable affirmation of your ministry always feels good. Sometimes you don't get a thank you or even a nod of appreciation. Keep going and know that you have done and lived your best for Jesus, and this will be your internal, and eternal reward.

Chapter 27

Your Service Options

For most of my life, preaching has been my calling, passion, hobby, and my world. Winning souls to Christ, baptizing people, and growing the church was not just a job for me but was an internal calling. It was a longing put inside me that would not let me go. I was willing to live in small modest houses, rent apartments, and work for almost nothing to have the opportunity to talk about Jesus. If you are called by God then you understand. "[18]Then they called them in again and commanded them not to speak or teach at all in the name of Jesus. [19]But Peter and John replied, "Which is right in God's eyes: to listen to you, or to him? You be the judges! [20]As for us, we cannot help speaking about what we have seen and heard." Acts 4: 18-20

Looking back, I would gather my family together and prayerfully consider a town where we all thought we might enjoy living. We would move to that town and start a church from scratch and let God take the church where he would want it to go. I would plan to spend my entire life with that congregation.

People have been starting their own churches and ministry organizations for a long time. Not everyone wants to attend a church where the pastor or ministry leader has solidified his or her position. Therefore, some people will never attend or will drop out if they feel they cannot gain some control. It's okay. Let them leave.

You must certainly share the ministry with others. Give the music, the small groups, the discipleship, the daily ministries to the people. Let them have ownership of God's work. This is the only way the church will grow. If you try to run everything then you will be the only one in attendance. However, maintain your presence in your pulpit and teaching/preaching ministry. You obviously will give insight and leadership to the entire ministry but you have to build an organization that has the freedom to grow.

What if the church or ministry you start remains small? Small ministries are not bad. You still have someplace to preach and serve every week. If you preach a few sermons that aren't so great then you can still go home in peace because no one is going to fire you. They might quit coming and giving their money but you have your pulpit so you can go back and try again. When you start your own church or ministry people will come and go and they might all leave, but at least your position is secure.

You can successfully grow your church. People are looking for a church that cares, preaches the Bible, loves people, and allows them to participate in the various ministries. You can build an organization that is inclusive of people from music, to youth, children, and seniors. Consider starting an elementary Christian school and even a junior high and high school. If you do, your church will be filled on Sunday. You can begin with a preschool, kindergarten, and then keep growing into the elementary classes. Utilize these children and families in your Sunday morning worship and your house will always be full. If you are in a traditional church you may have to spend your entire life selling this idea or any other idea to a group of people who simply prefer not to do anything but maintain the church cemetery and have potluck dinners. There are various ways to grow a ministry. At least if you are in charge then you and God and other visionaries who will join with you can go forward with the kingdom's work. Typically, in a traditional church, you have to obtain everyone's approval before you can start a new class or adjust the order of worship. Change is always a process in a traditional church. You simply must learn and follow the process. Every ministry and church will vary in style.

There are multiple other ministries that you can start, grow, and build. You can build a great youth ministry, senior adult ministry, children's ministry, a Christian preschool, elementary or high school. People are growing great counseling ministries today. You may start and develop a great evangelistic outreach ministry. You may develop your own non-profit ministry that feeds and helps people with human needs. What about starting and building an Emergency Response Ministry that helps others in times of disaster? You might consider a ministry in sales and marketing Christian materials and products. If you can think it then you are halfway to bringing your idea to fruition. Be creative. Do the ministry that you feel called to do. Be involved in the kind of ministry that you wake up in the morning excited to do.

Starting your own ministry comes with sacrifice. It is not easy. Sometimes it does not work out. The idea of going to a church with several hundred people attending and a nice facility is very difficult to turn down. You already have the financing in place. You do not have to worry about raising your salary. It can be very comfortable for a long time. Just be aware it is never forever. The day will come when you will feel pressured to move on or feel forced to retire or to resign. When this happens, there is nothing comfortable or enjoyable about the place you gave five, ten, or twenty years of your heart to. If you were in your own church for that many years, no one would be firing you. Instead, they would have to leave and find another church. It is easier for your deacons or leadership to find another church down the street than for you to uproot your family and move to another town after so many years.

What about all the thousands and thousands of existing churches and ministries? They need pastors, staff members, associates, and lots of workers. They are all looking for men and women called of God to help them. You and many others will serve these churches and help them to fulfill their mission. The chances are good that God will use you in a great way and your time with them will be exhilarating and fulfilling. If no one served all the current churches that exist today they would all eventually die. This would be tragic.

There is something so very special about being called to serve in a church ministry. Meeting the people, going through the process of being interviewed, and the voting process can be very exciting. Starting fresh with a new congregation and working with them to minister to people and reach people for Christ is thrilling. I never accepted a church that I was not grateful for and excited about serving. I always accepted the call with the commitment to give it my best in every capacity of ministry that I was expected and called to do. You should do the same. Wherever you are called to serve, go with 100% commitment to do and be your best for Jesus. Would I accept a pastoral position at this stage in my life? I might. It is up to God. At this stage of my life, I don't believe I feel called to start a church because there are so many churches that need pastors and staff. It would be easier at this stage to simply plug into a place and go to preaching and winning souls for Christ. However, I would never, say never. Again, it is up to God.

You need to pray now and talk to God about all of this. This book has given you something to think about. The goal in writing this is to stimulate your thinking and to help you and your family, your daily life, as well as your present and future ministry. Ministers seldom have mentors or advisors to give them good counsel. Often the minister is on his or her own trying to find or feel their way through their ministries, their personal lives, their decisions, and their calling. It is not always easy. Be real with God. Be real with yourself, with who you are, and with where you want to be in life and ministry. Talk to your family and include them. Talk and work together. They are in the middle of your ministry as much as you are and feel the joys as well as the pressures.

Chapter 28

Make the Best of Your Life

The minister lives a life of highs and some lows. When it is great, it is great, and when it is not so good, it can be difficult. No one lives a life of looking forward to the lows. We like the happiness and the thrill of the highs.

Like Isaiah in 40:31, we want to soar on wings like eagles filled with joy, new adventures, and rising above the daily grinds, challenges, and fiery darts that come our way.

Ministry, like any other work, must be lived day by day. All we have is the present. Every day is a gift, that is why it is called the present. Yesterday is in the past never to be relived, and tomorrow is only a hope and a promise that might never be experienced. So, we must live and love today.

Today must be lived where you are and with what you have in your life. Whatever might happen tomorrow, will be greatly affected by how you live life today. What might you be doing in 12 or 24 months if you make some decisions in the right direction today? Motivational speakers often ask about your five-year plan. A five-year plan is important, but we also need six-month and 12-month goals. Often, more can be accomplished in shorter increments. A long-term goal broken down into shorter incremental goals is more easily achievable.

For example, if you want to baptize 24 people in a year, it is easier to work toward baptizing two a month. If you need five new Bible study groups in your church, you would be wise to only start one every three or four months and nurture them into stability before beginning the next one. If your personal goal is to save $6000 a year for retirement or to purchase a house, then you will need to save $500 a month. Every month you will need to set aside and sacrifice to accomplish your goal. Always set goals that are within your grasp. The goal needs to be enough to be worthwhile but should not be so overwhelming that it is impossible to accomplish. The key is making decisions that take you in the right direction.

One of the ways education works is one class at a time. When you consider how many books you have to read or how many papers you have to write, you might become discouraged. You take it one page at a time. Reading a book is one page at a time. Writing a paper is one page at a time. Life is one minute, hour, and day at a time. If you do not like your life today, you have to set the wheels of change into motion. That may mean education, job applications, building your credentials, and proving yourself in daily life. The best way to move to a different ministry job is to do a great job where you are serving now. People like to hire success. If you do nothing where you are working now, and have nothing to show for your months or years of work, then what will you have to offer to whoever interviews you next?

Wherever you are and whatever you are doing today, be content, be happy, and make the best of it. When I started out preaching at the age of 16, I was ready to preach to large stadiums of people like Billy Graham was doing. I had the passion, the energy, and the desire to preach the gospel to the multitudes. But as a young, green, inexperienced, uneducated newly called minister, my opportunities were to preach to very small rural churches. However, that's exactly where I belonged. Those people were great to me and extended all the patience in the world.

When you are young, you are filled with zeal to do bigger and better things. Sometimes, the desire is to move forward quickly to a bigger church or larger ministry. Bigger looks better in every way. More people, more prestige, more salary, and often better housing and all that leads to even bigger and better opportunities down the road. I am not saying this is bad. This is all very human, and it is what the world places on our plates and in our minds. Sometimes bigger is better, and sometimes it is just more headaches. You never know until you get there. If you do get there, as in the place you left, you have to make the best of the bigger and better things that you have taken on. There will be more hospital visits, nursing homes, funerals and weddings, more meetings, more expectations, and more places where you are expected to be.

Wherever you are and whatever you are doing at this moment, find the peace of God which passes all understanding, Philippians 4:7. The peace of God today is like a balm of soothing contentment for your aching heart.

Everyone has days when they wonder when and how life will ever change. It will, and so much faster than we can imagine. Life changes so fast that we blink and cannot believe yesterday is so far, far away. That is why you need to savor your life today. You may be living in a little church parsonage. It won't be forever. You may be working as a volunteer or for a very low wage. You may feel underused and underappreciated. You may feel like your life, talents, and skills are going to waste. Do what you can do today. Do what you know to do today and look around you to enjoy and appreciate all that is at your fingertips today.

Life is always right in front of us. The situations of life present different and new opportunities. The situation you are in today presents you with an opportunity that tomorrow may not afford. If and when tomorrow comes, you make look back and think, "I should have done such and such yesterday while I had the opportunity." Thus, today's opportunities are different. Do what you can today.

An old saying is blossom where you are planted, and you will be transplanted. Be a good student. Be a good associate. Be a good team player. Be a worker. Be a good preacher. Be a hard worker. Be great to your family and loved ones. Be faithful at whatever you are doing and feel called to do. Jim Elliot said, "Wherever you are, be all there."

Live a life of common sense. God has not called you to be stupid. He does not want you doing things that will lead to the destruction of your life and ministry. God wants you to protect yourself and to run the race with patience, laying aside every weight and every sin that entangles us, looking unto Jesus the author and finisher of our faith, Hebrews 12: 1-3. Keep your mind and heart right with God. Keep your marriage right with God. Keep your family first and foremost. Be a good student of the word and a good worker of God among his people.

Often you will be faithful, work hard, and do all the right things but still not experience great success. That happens. God has not called us to be successful. He has called us to be faithful. Do the best you can do and trust God for the results. However, if you follow the plan of being faithful, working hard, and doing the right things, you certainly have a greater chance of experiencing success. If you throw the rule book out the window and do everything wrong, then failure is most likely to be your experience. You do not want that. Keep Galatians 6:9 in front of you, "Let us not become weary in doing good, for at the proper time we will reap a harvest if we do not give up."

I heard the story about the little train that traveled the United States from East to West and North to South. The train's travels were incredible and beautiful as it passed breathtaking scenery along the way. The freedoms of the trips were almost unlimited except that the train had one problem. That one problem was being bound by the track. For years the train passed by a beautiful lake that was so beautiful, clean, and appealing. The train saw people boating, fishing, and playing in the lake. The train felt slighted that it was prohibited from the refreshing feel of the lovely lake water. After many trips and many pangs of jealousy and resentment, the train made a decision one day to cast all reason aside. The train left the track and plunged directly into the lake. Once in the lake, the train realized that all it had ever known, experienced, and lived for would forever be a memory, in the past. Never again would it travel freely from East to West and North to South. Never again would it enjoy the sights and sounds of the Western Plains, The Rockies, or Smoky mountains. The farmlands of Mid America and the great rivers that it had once crossed would never be experienced again. Forevermore, all the train would know would be a long and dismal life of being submerged in the quagmire at the bottom of what seemed to be such an inviting lake. Now, it's existence would be to rust out and eventually die because it decided to leave the track.

Making the best of ministry and experiencing contentment in your life will hinge on the decisions that you make most every day. Most of what you do, will never be recognized in this world. You are not going to receive an Oscar or a Tony award for your faithfulness in visiting sick people at the hospital. You are not going to earn an Academy award for visiting the elderly shut-ins or the nursing home. You are not going to receive a Nobel Peace Prize for the hours you spend on your knees in prayer for a lost soul to be saved. You probably aren't going to receive too many, if any, standing ovations for the messages that you spent hours preparing for, putting your heart on a platter for, and serving up to your congregation. There will be hours and even a life of sacrifice where you will make decisions every day that will not receive much if any recognition. However, do not lose sight of this scripture, Matthew 25:23, "His master replied, 'Well done, good and faithful servant! You have been faithful with a few things; I will put you in charge of many things. Come and share your master's happiness!" And then there is 1 Corinthians 15:58, "Therefore, my dear brothers and sisters, stand firm. Let nothing move you. Always give yourselves fully to the work of the Lord, because you know that your labor in the Lord is not in vain." Hebrews 12: 1-2 reminds us that we are compassed about with so great a cloud of witnesses."

I heard an old preacher say, "The person who loves God most will be at his post when all the others have walked away." That is a decision to be faithful. To stand true and stick with what God has called you to do. It is not always easy, and it is not always rewarded, in this world.

The chances of life going well for you are better than if you decide to throw all caution to the wind. There is the roadmap of God's word, the Sermon on the Mount, The Ten Commandments, The Golden Rule, the still small voice of the Holy Spirit, and Christ-filled commonsense that will guide you along your journey. There is a track that will take you so many, many places. There is a track of safety. There is also a track of good decisions that will fill your life with peace and contentment. You may not always have a shiny new car, and there may be material sacrifices that you will experience along the way, but I am talking about peace of mind. I am talking about the peace of God that fills our hearts. A peace that the world cannot give and the world cannot take away. This inner peace that will flood your heart and family is greater, and better than anything that you might consider jumping off the track for in your life and ministry. Philippians 4:7, "And the peace of God, which passeth all understanding, shall keep your hearts and minds through Christ Jesus." John 14:27. [27]Peace I leave with you; my peace I give you. I do not give to you as the world gives. Do not let your hearts be troubled and do not be afraid."

Part of making the best of life and your ministry and experiencing contentment is making good decisions. A man was once thinking about putting a shirt on and asked his wife, "Honey, is this shirt clean or dirty?" She replied, "If you have to ask, it's dirty." Often there will be invitations and opportunities that will come your way. Many will be those that you will walk through easily, joyfully, and without reluctance. You will know that it is okay, and you will feel God's freedom and power. There will be other opportunities that will be the equivalent of the train leaving the track. Once you decide that, it is fatal, and whatever freedom and joy you experienced in the past will have been tossed aside.

Keep in mind, "If God be for us who can be against us," Romans 8:31. God gives us the playbook of his word to follow. There is freedom, and there is liberty in Jesus. The truth of Jesus sets us free. Serve God in power, freedom, and truth. Do not let the world or even a mean group of superficial evil religious people imprison you. The beautiful track of God is long, and the possibilities of serving him are endless and unlimited. What God and you can accomplish together is often beyond the minds of those who might try to limit you, enslave you or even stomp out your service and ministry for Jesus. You and God must work all this out in your calling and life for him. God is greater than all his enemies. He is greater than all the world. He made the heavens and the earth, and he has made the most unique creation of all, and this is you. He made you. He also has carved out your calling and your ministry. Do not let others shape your ministry. Do not be a carbon copy of someone else. Be you. Be who God created you to be. Do not spend your life trying to fit into someone else's plan. Fit into God's plan. Before your life is over, be you and be who God created you to be. You do not have to jump out of an airplane without a parachute to fulfill this. Follow the leading of God, and God will work through you to accomplish great things for him.

CPSIA information can be obtained
at www.ICGtesting.com
Printed in the USA
BVHW031048030321
601587BV00020B/216/J